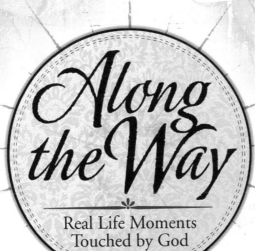

## Along the Way

Real Life Moments
Touched by God

# FOR TEENS

Meredith® Books
Des Moines, Iowa

**Jordan
House**™

1716 Locust Street
Des Moines, Iowa 50309-3023
meredithbooks.com

Printed in China

**Along the Way**
First Edition.
Library of Congress Control Number:
ISBN 978-0-696-23399-9

Produced with the assistance of The Livingstone Corporation. General editors: Betsy Schmitt,
Linda Washington. Project staff: Ashley Taylor, Greg Longbons, Linda Taylor, Larry Taylor,
Kirk Luttrell.

Cover photograph copyright iStockphoto®, Christian Nitu.

# TABLE OF CONTENTS

Introduction . . . . . . . . . . . . . . . . . . . . . . . . . . . . . . . . . . . . . . . . . . . . . . . 5

1. My Three Minutes of Glory—*Persisting Past Failure* . . . . . . . . . . . . . . . . . . . 7

2. View from the Bench—*Learning the True Source of Wisdom* . . . . . . . . . . . . . . 11

3. Expectations—*Approaching God with Your Frustrations and Desires* . . . . . . . . . . 14

4. Peace as a Masterpiece—*Discovering True Perfection* . . . . . . . . . . . . . . . . . . 18

5. Making It Right—*Finding Reconciliation Before God* . . . . . . . . . . . . . . . . 22

6. So You Had a Bad Day—*Discovering God in the Details* . . . . . . . . . . . . . . . 26

7. Cutting Through the Pain—*Learning How Much God Loves You* . . . . . . . . . . . 29

8. The Raging Fire—*Discovering the Value of Watching Your Words* . . . . . . . . . . . 32

9. The World's Worst Driver—*Learning God's Compassion Through Failure* . . . . . . . 35

10. Paid in Full—*Experiencing the Joy of a Debt Forgiven* . . . . . . . . . . . . . . . 39

11. My Wake-Up Call—*Being Reconciled After Rebellion* . . . . . . . . . . . . . . . . 43

12. My Stepdad and Me—*Coping with a Difficult Relationship* . . . . . . . . . . . . . 47

13. A Drive to Remember—*Obeying God's Principles* . . . . . . . . . . . . . . . . . . . 50

14. Letting Go of Eric—*Moving Beyond the Heartthrob to True Love* . . . . . . . . . . 53

15. An Attitude Adjustment—*Admitting a Need to Change* . . . . . . . . . . . . . . . 57

16. Happy New Year—*Celebrating a Restored Life* . . . . . . . . . . . . . . . . . . . . . 61

17. A Baptism of Rain—*Exploring the Reality of God's Presence* . . . . . . . . . . . . . 64

18. A Change of Direction—*Going Beyond Life's Impasses* . . . . . . . . . . . . . . . . 68

19. A Horse Story—*Sharing One Another's Burdens* . . . . . . . . . . . . . . . . . . . . 71

20. The Way Less Traveled—*Finding My Path in the Road of Pain* . . . . . . . . . . . 74

21. Lip Service—*Combining Faith and Action* . . . . . . . . . . . . . . . . . . . . . . . . 78

22. Sheep, Goats, and a Pair of Shoes—*Learning the Truth About God's Kingdom* . . . . 82

23. Birds Don't Gallop and Horses Don't Sing— *Learning to Accept Yourself* . . . . . . 85

24. Harvesting Joy—*Trusting God in Times of Change* . . . . . . . . . . . . . . . . . . 89

25. Have You Ever Been in Love?—*Mending a Broken Heart* . . . . . . . . . . . . . . . 93

26. The Real Deal—*Watching a Life of Authentic Faith* . . . . . . . . . . . . . . . . . . 97

27. It's All True—*Endings Mean Beginnings Too* . . . . . . . . . . . . . . . . . . . . . . 100

28. In Search of Water—*Thirsting to Know Jesus* . . . . . . . . . . . . . . . . . . . . . . 103

29. House of Hope—*Finding a Miracle in a Disaster* . . . . . . . . . . . . . . . . . . . 106

30. A Reason to Play—*Finding Joy in Discipline* . . . . . . . . . . . . . . . . . . . . . . 109

31. Who Is He?—*Discovering a Father Who Knows All Secrets* . . . . . . . . . . . . . . 112

32. Empty Stockings, Full Hearts—*Seeing Life from God's Perspective* . . . . . . . . . . 116

33. A Coyote for Christmas—*Sharing the Gift of God's Love* . . . . . . . . . . . . . . . 120

34. Who Am I?—*Finding Your Identity Through the Love of God* . . . . . . . . . . . . . 124

35. God in the Bullring—*Knowing You Are Not Alone* . . . . . . . . . . . . . . . . . . 128

36. Making Plans—*Learning to Cooperate with God* . . . . . . . . . . . . . . . . . . . . . . . . . . .132

37. Does Jesus Really Love Me?—*Overcoming Bulimia* . . . . . . . . . . . . . . . . . . . . . .136

38. Wrestling with Faith—*Reaching Out Instead of Judging*. . . . . . . . . . . . . . . . . . . .140

39. In This Together—*Appreciating the Community of Believers* . . . . . . . . . . . . . . . . .144

40. Taking the Heat—*Watching God Work in Difficult Times* . . . . . . . . . . . . . . . . .147

41. Taking the High Road—*Learning to Rely on God* . . . . . . . . . . . . . . . . . . . . . . . .151

42. Not So Far Away—*Meeting the God Who Sees All* . . . . . . . . . . . . . . . . . . . . . . . .154

43. An Embarrassing Moment—*Putting God's Love to Practical Use* . . . . . . . . . . . . . .158

44. The Lifting—*Defeating the Giants of Life* . . . . . . . . . . . . . . . . . . . . . . . . . . . . . .162

45. Ahead of the Game—*Developing a Leader's Voice* . . . . . . . . . . . . . . . . . . . . . . . .165

46. Abstinence Road—*Trusting in God's Safeguards* . . . . . . . . . . . . . . . . . . . . . . . . .169

47. Are You Qualified?—*Trusting the Spirit's Guidance When Telling Others About God* . . . .172

48. A Whole New Dream—*Giving Up Our Plans in Favor of God's Plans* . . . . . . . . . .175

49. Fear Has a Purpose—*Allowing the Fear of God to Mold Character* . . . . . . . . . . . .179

50. The Grizzly and the Air-Conditioner—*Experiencing the Grace of God* . . . . . . . . .181

51. A Musical Moment—*Reaching Out Through Music* . . . . . . . . . . . . . . . . . . . . . . .184

52. The "Boring" Life—*Discovering the Power of Living for Christ* . . . . . . . . . . . . . . .187

53. Lost in God—*Finding Friendship and Hope through God's Love*. . . . . . . . . . . . . . .190

54. Burnt Shoes—*Discovering God's Imprint* . . . . . . . . . . . . . . . . . . . . . . . . . . . . . .193

55. Shooting Basketballs, Not Bullets—*Demolishing the Lines Between Enemies*. . . . . .196

56. Arms Wide Open—*Meeting Jesus Through a Stranger* . . . . . . . . . . . . . . . . . . . . .200

57. Busy and Broken—*Trusting God to Fill the Emptiness*. . . . . . . . . . . . . . . . . . . . .204

58. Dealing with Darkness—*Overcoming Anger and Bitterness* . . . . . . . . . . . . . . . . .208

59. Invisible—*Believing That God Knows You* . . . . . . . . . . . . . . . . . . . . . . . . . . . . .212

60. A Lesson in Laughter—*Learning to Laugh at Oneself* . . . . . . . . . . . . . . . . . . . . .216

61. Down and Out—*Asking for Help in Tough Times* . . . . . . . . . . . . . . . . . . . . . . . .219

62. The Great Date Wait—*Waiting for God's Choice*. . . . . . . . . . . . . . . . . . . . . . . . .223

63. Keep Going!—*Persisting in Faith* . . . . . . . . . . . . . . . . . . . . . . . . . . . . . . . . . . . .227

64. A Matter of Perspective—*Finding God in Real Life*. . . . . . . . . . . . . . . . . . . . . . .230

65. Tomorrow's Choices Today—*Learning to Be a Leader* . . . . . . . . . . . . . . . . . . . . .234

66. A Poolside Chat—*Coming Alongside a Friend*. . . . . . . . . . . . . . . . . . . . . . . . . . .237

67. Not Finished Yet—*Crying Out to God When He's All You Have Left*. . . . . . . . . . . .241

Author Bios. . . . . . . . . . . . . . . . . . . . . . . . . . . . . . . . . . . . . . . . . . . . . . . . . . . . . . .245

Topical Index. . . . . . . . . . . . . . . . . . . . . . . . . . . . . . . . . . . . . . . . . . . . . . . . . . . . . .249

Scripture Index . . . . . . . . . . . . . . . . . . . . . . . . . . . . . . . . . . . . . . . . . . . . . . . . . . . .254

# INTRODUCTION

Many, many years ago a young man beginning his journey into adulthood listened carefully to some words of advice: *Trust in the Lord with all your heart; do not depend on your own understanding. Seek his will in all you do, and he will show you which path to take.*

After all, a young person has so many choices. Sometimes the life-roads ahead of you can look like a complicated freeway interchange with underpasses and overpasses converging, overlapping, and curving in all directions. And as you learned when you first started driving a car, if you turn onto the wrong road returning to the right route can be a confusing, even dangerous process.

That young man long ago learned he didn't have to make his journey alone. He could find help from others who traveled the road with him and from others who were further along the way than he was. And best of all he could trust God to provide direction for every mile ahead.

The young man followed that timeless advice, written in Proverbs 3:5-6. As a result God directed his path to become the leader of the greatest nation in his world, Israel, and to be the wisest person who ever lived.

God loves helping young people along their way. That's what this book is all about. You'll read stories about teenagers who found that God was with them as they navigated the roads of life—on a pleasant drive, through a bedeviling storm, or amid unfamiliar interchanges. Following each story the *When God Breaks Through* section gives tips to help you become a more seasoned spiritual traveler. And you can learn how to apply those spiritual truths to your own journey through each *My Challenge* section.

So don't trek alone. Walk the road with others who can give you help, hope, and inspiration as you journey *Along the Way*.

## persisting **PAST** failure

From my first day of kindergarten, I was always the last one picked for any game or sport that required any athletic ability. It was humiliating to always be at the end of the line. In fourth grade my friend Donna was in a cast and on crutches and *she* got picked before me! That was a *really* bad day!

I hated gym class and recess, finding any excuse to avoid the embarrassment that came with choosing teams. I dug into my studies instead. I figured if God didn't give me athletic talents, I should at least use the academic ones he did give me. The problem with that? Smart kids with no athletic ability are even more unpopular!

A few weeks before my freshman year began I saw an announcement in our local newspaper for junior varsity volleyball tryouts. For a small town "tryouts" meant showing up at the gym, picking out a uniform that fit, and finding a partner to practice with. Do that and you're in!

I bravely went to the tryouts. When I walked onto the gym floor, the coach's expressionless face told the whole story. She'd been my gym teacher since third grade, and she knew my athletic ability was severely lacking! In a small high school of only 120 students, everyone was pretty much guaranteed a spot, so she was practically forced to include me on the team.

I never missed a practice, usually showing up early to gain a few extra points in her eyes. I worked as hard as the other girls, but I was always far behind them in my skills. Several weeks into the season, I was still serving underhand while the others had perfected their overhand serves and were showing the promise needed to move to the varsity team. But I didn't give up. I knew I wasn't good, but I really wanted to be a part of the team.

During my first season on the team I made a point here and there, but that was it. I decided to try again my sophomore year. Again I stepped on the gym floor with a grin. Again Coach Flescher raised her eyebrows in my direction and her face went pale.

"You're back," she said. "Take a spot along the wall."

She still hated having me around, and I was still bad. Yep, this was going to be a great year!

Four weeks into the season, my skills were no better than they were my freshman year. My underhanded serves brought giggles from my teammates and the varsity girls.

"God, please make this better!" I cried out one night alone in the locker room. "I know I'm not that good, but it hurts to be laughed at. I'm really trying."

The next week God answered my prayer.

Our team was on the road, playing in a conference matchup against Barneveld, and I exerted my usual effort. I didn't make any points, but I returned a few serves and helped keep our team alive. After three games, we were done. Many of the girls went home with their parents, but I stayed to watch the varsity games.

**She still hated having me around, and I was still bad. Yep, this was going to be a great year!**

That's when the unexpected happened. For some reason the varsity team's bench was nearly empty. Clearly they wouldn't have enough girls on the team for regulation play. When the coach realized what was happening, she hung her head. She repeatedly scanned the gymnasium. On her third pass her eyes met mine. She closed her eyes, shook her head, and probably swore under her breath.

"Heidi, you're on the bench!" she said with disgust. "Hurry up!"

Was she kidding? Apparently not!

Two and a half games into the match, I was still enjoying my warm spot on the end of the wooden bench. This varsity thing wasn't so bad. I got to be part of the team and didn't have to play. Now *this* was a team sport I enjoyed.

Caught up in my moment, I didn't hear the coach yelling. "Heidi! You're serving!"

"I'm what?"

"Serving! Get out there!" she said, grabbing my arm. "We need four points to win. Don't mess this up. Just serve the ball, get it over the net, and rotate around the court. Don't do anything more than that. Let the other girls do the work."

Wow, she just bled confidence right out of me!

I was terrified as I sauntered to the floor. Carla, a junior standing next to me in the rotation, leaned against my shoulder and harshly whispered, "Don't screw up this game, Heidi."

I was shaking as I got ready to serve. *I don't know how to serve overhand like the rest of the girls on this team. This should be neat!*

I closed my eyes and with the best underhand serve I could muster, I hit that ball. And it went over the net. Wow! It went over the net! It never did that for me!

The other team spiked it back right into the net. Score a point for our team. That was great until I realized I had to serve again. I closed my eyes and punched the ball with every ounce of power I had.

One more point.

High fives came to me from girls who normally didn't know I existed. But I didn't have time to bask in the glory of my success yet. We still needed two points to win.

"God, if you've ever been there for me, be there now," I whispered.

I served. One more point. Only one to go!

The crowd was screaming and the coach was on her feet. I don't know what she was saying. I figured it was best if I didn't hear her. So far I was doing OK on my own.

For the final time I held out the ball, closed my eyes, and hit it. The ball barely cleared the net, but it did. That's all that mattered. And the other team punched it, trying to get it back on our court. They failed.

Game over! We'd just won! *I'd* just won!

The varsity girls surrounded me, giving me hugs and high fives, and then carried me off the floor to the locker room for a celebratory shower in my uniform. I wasn't thrilled with that, but if it meant I had gained their respect for the night, I could live with it.

The cheers continued as we danced to the bus.

The parents. The students. The team. They were all so proud of me. Nobody, though, was prouder of me than me!

I had dealt with adversity for so long. It felt good to finally be a real part of a team—a team that I never played on again. That was all I needed to feel validated. Just four points. That's all.

God had heard my prayers. He saw my struggles and my persistence. He knew how my feelings were continually hurt. And he gave me three minutes of glory that took away 10 years of pain. God really smiled on me that night.

*Heidi J. Krumenauer*

# WHEN GOD
## breaks through

When you want something badly, you probably do whatever it takes to get it. Heidi persisted at a sport because she wanted to be part of the team. Do you sometimes wish your goal could be achieved instantly? But persistence means really working at something to achieve a goal. James, Jesus' brother, gave props to those who persist: "We praise the ones who endured the most. You remember how patient Job was and how the Lord finally helped him. The Lord did this because he is so merciful and kind" (James 5:11, CEV).

## my
## CHALLENGE

What goals have you set recently? How do your actions show your willingness to persist until your goal is reached? If you can't think of any recent actions, how about setting a new goal: to persist.

# VIEW FROM THE BENCH 2

## learning the **TRUE SOURCE** of wisdom

I thought it would be the trip of a lifetime. This was our annual varsity soccer trip to Ohio. Eighteen of us crammed into two tiny vans and hit the road. No one could have been more excited than I was, and not just because we were going to play soccer the whole time. Because this was my senior year in the Christian school, I wanted to make the best of this last trip with the team.

Outside our hotel the coach read room assignments and I learned I would stay with Josh, Wes, and Bryan. They were three of the best athletes on our team. Hanging out with them would be fantastic!

*I'll learn a lot from them about soccer,* I figured.

Best of all, they genuinely seemed thrilled to have me along. As we rode up the elevator discussing the weekend, they included me in the conversation as if I'd known them forever. I decided the weekend would be a time to make new friends and forge stronger spiritual bonds with my Christian brothers. However, this vision collapsed only a few hours later.

We all gathered to play games and practice juggling soccer balls for a few hours. Then around 11:30, everyone headed to bed. After all we had a doubleheader the following day.

Just after I returned to the room, Josh, Bryan, and Wes entered with a grocery bag. They pulled some beers out of it and asked if I wanted one. Even after I declined, they kept pushing it. It would have been so easy for me to grab a beer. I knew they'd accept me better, but I knew I had to pass. Then they pulled out the chewing tobacco, and I had to say "no" again.

Later that night as I was lying in bed, I realized I was frustrated with God. I thought my aggravation was because having a beer with those guys would have been so much easier than sticking by my God-given convictions. I'd barely dozed off to sleep when I was awakened by the sound of vomiting coming from the bathroom. So much for learning about soccer from them.

The next day Josh, Bryan, and Wes all started for both games; I, on the other hand, received 10 minutes of playing time. As I sat on the bench watching the guys play and wondering if they still felt sick from the night before, my soul continued to bristle with aggravation.

Suddenly I realized the real reason I was angry: God allowed these star athletes to continue to play the game they loved even though they were hypocrites about their Christianity. Meanwhile I was trying to live what I believed and followed the team rules, and I sat on the bench. I felt betrayed and confused.

**I'd barely dozed off to sleep when I was awakened by the sound of vomiting coming from the bathroom.**

I dealt with the unfairness of the situation for a couple of weeks. One morning everyone was at school waiting for soccer practice to begin—everyone except Josh, Bryan, and Wes. A few minutes later we learned they'd been caught garage-hopping for beer, and had been suspended for two weeks. They wouldn't be allowed to play in the state finals.

I can still see the expressions on their faces when they found out the consequences for their behavior. I had to sympathize with the crushing disappointment they showed.

From the whole incident I came to the conclusion not only that what goes around comes around, but everybody sins. I thought I would gain incredible wisdom from these guys and felt disappointed that I didn't receive any. But I did learn that God is the source of all wisdom. Only God's truth is real.

*Stephen Tracy*

# WHEN GOD
## breaks through

Maybe you've been disappointed by someone you thought was cool, but who turned out to be not at all what you expected—and not a model worth emulating or looking to for advice. Stephen ultimately realized that God was the source of wisdom. David, the Old Testament king who often learned life lessons the hard way, also discovered this fact. That's why he could say, "Fear of the Lord is the foundation of true wisdom. All who obey his commandments will grow in wisdom" (Psalm 111:10, NLT).

## my
## CHALLENGE

Think about the people you usually turn to for advice. How does God's advice, which you can gain through reading the Bible and through others' wise counsel, compare with theirs? If you're not sure, take a moment to write down some of the advice you've received lately. Now grab your Bible (preferably one with a concordance) and see how the advice you've been given matches with Scripture.

# EXPECTATIONS 3

## approaching **GOD** with your frustrations and desires

I stomped into my bedroom, knelt down, and plopped two pieces of paper onto the bed. I looked to my left at the blue rocker and thought about all the Christian romance novels I'd read sitting in that rocker or lying on this bed. I thought about all the homework I'd done in this room. My lap desk sat in the corner waiting. But homework wasn't on the agenda today, nor was a good romance novel. *I can't escape reality any more. I have to do something*, I thought.

I looked at the two pieces of paper on the bed. One, a brochure from Southwestern Baptist University in Bolivar, Missouri, boasted happy college students engaged in study and fun. Inside it outlined the college's special features from the intimate feel of the campus to the variety of social and academic choices. The colorful images leaped off the page to draw prospective students into college life. But my real problem was the other piece of paper: a letter from Baylor University.

When I visited Baylor with my parents my junior year in high school it felt right. The other two schools we visited hadn't impressed us at all. But Baylor? Everything about it seemed to chant "You belong here, you belong here." Strong academics, a Christian atmosphere, and the right distance from home. It had it all. But I didn't.

Grades? Good enough. Scholastic Aptitude Test scores? Just fine. Financial aid? A big fat zero. My father apparently made too much money for my family to qualify for financial aid, but not enough to pay for a college education at Baylor. So I stared at the acceptance letter from Baylor that I'd had for more

ALONG THE WAY

than six months. It was *April* and *nothing* had happened to pave my way to attend Baylor.

My parents were somewhat apologetic after exhausting all potential financial aid resources. I'd prayed over the months for God to send some assistance. I knew my mom had prayed a lot. But no money and it was *April*. I'd have to make a decision soon.

So here I sat and considered the college a friend from church suggested. Baylor is only an hour and a half away—close enough to come home anytime, but far enough that no one would expect me to come home a lot. Southwestern Baptist University is cheaper, but it seemed so small and was farther away. Baylor seemed just right for me to make some

**"OK, God. This is it. You know I don't have any money to go."**

changes in my life and find somewhere to fit in. I almost started to cry, but remembered my agenda for the day: to *do* something.

I arranged the papers on the bed: SBU on the right and Baylor on the left. Still kneeling, I poured out my heart to God. "OK, God. This is it. You know I don't have any money to go. You know my parents don't have enough money to send me. And now I've heard about this other college. If it means that I'm supposed to go to this other college, then I need some clear direction. But I thought I was supposed to go to Baylor. So if I'm supposed to go to Baylor, please, this week, make it obvious." I got up, satisfied, and got ready for bed.

I woke up the next morning with no new revelations. No burning bushes or angels drifted down to point the way. I didn't know what to expect, but I did expect to have some answer during the next week.

"Letter for you, Shelley," my mom said when I got home from school that day. Her face showed apprehension. I frowned as she handed me the envelope from Baylor. I opened it carefully. I did pray for clear direction. Revoking my acceptance letter due to lack of funds could be one. Then again, maybe they'd taken pity on my family and offered me some grant money.

It started off, *Congratulations!* My heart skipped a beat as I continued to read, *On behalf of President Herbert H. Reynolds, we are pleased to name you as a recipient of a Presidential Scholarship at Baylor University.* Whoa! I skipped down to the amount, *$5,000 to be divided equally over your four undergraduate years.*

I paused and slumped into a chair. What did this mean? Yes, I got some money, but not enough. I tried to thank God, but was more confused than thankful. I continued to read the grade point average requirements and the fact that they sent an announcement to my local newspaper.

The fourth paragraph stated, *Also we are pleased to announce that your student account has been credited with funds from an anonymous source, which will cover your tuition, room, board, and books.*

*What?* I looked up from the letter at my mom, tears beginning in my eyes and turning into sobs. My mom rushed over to comfort me, but I stopped her with a huge hug and started shouting, "God is so *great!* Praise God!" and other phrases loud enough to let God in heaven know I was grateful and inspired by his awesome power and timing. And I silently promised that in the coming weeks whenever people asked or talked about college, I would tell them about God's provision.

*Shelley H. as told to David W. Barnett*

# WHEN GOD
## breaks through

Ever feel afraid to approach God with your frustrations, thinking he doesn't care enough to listen? We sometimes look at God as an extension of our parents, as someone who might get tired of hearing our complaints or who might answer in a way that reflects his or her weariness. But God never gets tired. This is why James could encourage believers to pray expectantly.

> *"If you need wisdom, ask our generous God, and he will give it to you. He will not rebuke you for asking. But when you ask him, be sure that your faith is in God alone. Do not waver, for a person with divided loyalty is as unsettled as a wave of the sea that is blown and tossed by the wind. Such people should not expect to receive anything from the Lord"* (James 1:5–7, NLT).

Shelley prayed honestly and expectantly. And God answered. Prayer gives God the green light to act on your behalf. When you feel stalled, pause and pray.

## my
## CHALLENGE

Have you talked to God about the situations or relationships that frustrate you? When you pray, do you expect God to answer? How has Shelley's experience affected the way you view God?

# PEACE AS A MASTERPIECE 4

## discovering **TRUE** perfection

"So, Lucy, Bill says you're anorexic."

I stared past the red PE shirt hanging in my gym locker before I closed the metal door. It was the first day of my freshman year in high school, and everyone in eighth period PE had received new locker assignments. Katie, one of my volleyball teammates from middle school, leaned against the adjoining locker chewing a wad of gum and staring at me.

"Um, what?" my face grew hot as my fingers fumbled to latch the combination lock. "Why did he say that?"

"You look a lot skinnier than last year, and Bill and some others say it's because you turned anorexic or something this summer." Katie rested her new algebra book on her hip and brushed her blonde hair behind her shoulder.

*No! People are supposed to think I look good, not spread rumors.*

I slid my pencil-thin arms through the straps of my bulging backpack and plastered a smile across my face. "I had the flu twice this summer and have had trouble putting weight back on. I also started running to get in shape for volleyball. That's all."

As I hurried out of the locker room, I glimpsed my reflection in a trophy case window. *Still ugly,* I thought, as I walked toward my mother's minivan. She, my father, and I were driving straight from school to the hospital.

Inside the hospital "Eating Disorder" ward, my toes curled as I stood on the icy scale for my weekly weigh-in. I'd been weighing in each week for 14 months—ever since my shocked parents had seen me in a swimsuit and realized how much weight I'd lost. But I wasn't getting any better. I didn't want to get better.

*Tap, tap, tap.* Dr. Sanders, my psychologist, tapped the black weight across the bar with his pen. Too far to the right, too heavy. *Tap, tap.* A little to the left. The balance teetered and steadied.

"Hmm," Dr. Sanders grimaced as he jotted down the number in my file. "Not good, kiddo. Not good. You're down—significantly."

I lowered my chin. I already knew I had not gained any weight. The garbage can had eaten my sack lunches all week. I shuffled back into Dr. Sanders' office, sinking into the scratchy, Herculon chair in the corner across from my parents. Eating disorder literature lined the walls in the cramped office.

My mother dabbed at her eyes behind her glasses with a crumpled tissue. Dad was quiet.

"OK, Lucy," Dr. Sanders closed the door and settled into his desk chair. His voice was stern. "Your parents and I have had patience—too much patience—with your minimal progress. We've told you that if you don't gain the necessary weight, we'll pull you from school and place you in the hospital so you'll receive the necessary calories to get to a healthy weight again."

My eyes burned as I stared at the carpeted floor. I heard my mother sniffling. *Why was she upset? Nobody was forcing her to gain weight.*

"Do you understand how serious we are, Lucy?" my dad asked. "At this weight, you're putting your heart at risk."

I didn't respond.

Dr. Sanders leaned back in his chair. "Your dad's right, Lucy. If you have not gained weight next week, you'll be admitted into the hospital."

I sat, numb from so many emotions. I felt confused, angry, scared, and abandoned. How had things gotten so out of control? How could Mom and Dad just put me in the hospital? I only wanted to be perfect. Why was that so wrong?

I tossed and turned in bed that night. 11:15 . . . 1:48 . . . 2:34. I turned the glowing face of my alarm clock toward the wall, and my hand brushed my Bible.

*Maybe reading will help me fall asleep.* I grabbed the Bible and the flashlight on my nightstand and let the pages fall open to Hebrews, where I had stuffed the previous week's Sunday school worksheets.

As I began to read, my eyes fell on Hebrews 10:14 (NIV), "Because by one sacrifice he has made perfect forever those who are being made holy." I read it again. And again. "By one sacrifice *he* has made perfect."

I closed the book. I had accepted Christ as my Savior when I was a little girl and remembered reading that verse before, but I never really thought about its meaning then.

"Jesus," I whispered. "I . . . I'm so scared. I've been trying so hard to be perfect—to make the best grades in my class, to play on the volleyball team, to hold offices in student council, and to be thin so I can look good and make friends. But I can't do it anymore. I hate how I look and feel and the way people are spreading rumors. No matter how hard I try, I can't make myself perfect. Only you can—that's what the verse means."

**I only wanted to be perfect. Why was that so wrong?**

I sat up in my covers, pulling my knees into my arms. "Jesus, I know that in your eyes, I am a masterpiece, but by hating the way I look, I've insulted you. Please forgive me, and please help me overcome this eating disorder. Please help me to remember that when you died on the cross, I was forgiven and made perfect. I am only perfect because of your forgiveness and grace."

As I finished praying, peace settled over me. It was as if Christ had lifted my burden for perfection with one hand and taken my hand in his other. I still had a challenging path ahead, but instead of depending on my own strength, I could depend on the Lord.

Over the next year I slowly began to regain the significant weight I had lost. It wasn't easy giving up control over my eating. I had to remind myself daily, even after I had overcome anorexia, that no matter how hard I tried to be perfect on my own, I could not attain that goal. If I could, there would have been no reason for Christ to die on the cross for me. It is only through God's grace and sacrifice am I considered perfect. God's creative design makes me a masterpiece.

*Lucy M. as told to Elizabeth Hubbard*

## WHEN GOD
### breaks through

Perfection is a game nobody can win. If you find yourself playing it, maybe you need to hear the words of Hebrews 10:14 again. Here's how it reads in *The Message:* "It was a perfect sacrifice by a perfect person to perfect some very imperfect people. By that single offering he did everything that needed to be done for everyone who takes part in the purifying process." Jesus, the only perfect person who ever lived, is in the business of perfecting—completing, changing—those who trust him. He takes all our imperfections and makes them perfect in God's eyes.

## my
## CHALLENGE

When do you feel most out of control? What do you usually do when that happens? If you're tired of playing the perfection game, talk to God. Tell him about the frustrations, anger, and disappointments you've experienced because of trying to be perfect at school, home, and with your friends. Ask him to help you surrender your struggles and allow him to be perfect for you.

## finding **RECONCILIATION** before God

"Hi, Ann. So why are you here today?" the doctor asked lightheartedly.

"Uh, well," I said. Then I burst into tears.

My doctor looked at me suspiciously. My family was among his first patients when he'd opened his new practice years earlier, so he remembered us without looking at our charts. I was what he called the All-American Girl—a nice kid from a nice family who's not into drugs or drinking. Of course in all my trips to get sports physicals or booster shots, I'd never cried. But this was a little more serious.

The doctor suddenly sat on his wheeled stool and sternly looked at me. His voice was deeper now, and quieter. He almost whispered when he asked again, "Why are you here?"

I couldn't even look up as I twisted my boyfriend's class ring around and around on my finger. The thumping in my stomach competed with the pounding of my heart. My thoughts dashed in a relay race.

*He'll hate me now. I've let him down. I'm such a disappointment. I'm going to get a lecture to beat all lectures. How do they test for pregnancy? Will it involve a needle?*

After several uncomfortable seconds, I told him I was afraid I was pregnant. So much for being an All-American girl. Without a word he rolled his stool away from the table and called a nurse to start the exam. They quickly determined that I was four months' pregnant.

Sadly I had given into the usual arguments: *If I really love him, this affection must be OK. Nothing will ever happen. Dave told me so.* Dave was my first serious boyfriend. We were considered one of the cutest couples in our 300-member high school class.

"So when are you going to tell your parents?" The doctor's look of anger and disappointment caused me to become very defensive. Then he went a question further: "And just what do you plan to do?"

"Dave and I are getting married and we'll tell our parents when we're ready." I couldn't believe I was being so brash.

"I'll give you 24 hours and then I'm calling them," he announced. I knew he meant it.

I left his office in a daze, knowing my life had just taken on a completely new role and definition.

My boyfriend of two years was surprisingly supportive and optimistic. I told him about the doctor's ultimatum, and Dave became a man before my eyes. He made plans to tell his parents and then to help me tell mine. He arrived at my house early that evening. Nervously we stood in the kitchen and asked my mom to join us.

**After several uncomfortable seconds, I told him I was afraid I was pregnant.**

With one long breath, I blurted out, "Mom, I'm pregnant and we're getting married."

That was so hard to say aloud, but it was out now and nothing could change me back to her innocent little girl.

She caught me off guard with her scream.

"What's wrong?" Dad demanded as he ran up from the basement.

"They're getting married! Ann's pregnant, and I'm throwing myself across the railroad tracks!" My mother screamed again.

This might not seem like a serious threat, but we actually lived next to railroad tracks. So I had my boyfriend listen for a train whistle while I called our pastor. He arrived within 10 minutes.

"What's going on here, Ann?" he asked as he looked at each of us in turn.

"We're getting married," I answered. I touched my boyfriend's shoulder. "I'm pregnant, and Mom is going to throw herself across the railroad tracks."

He cleared his throat and looked toward heaven, his lips rolling in and out.

Finally he looked at Dave and me with sincere concern. "I am going to talk to your parents in the living room. Meanwhile, you two go to the family room and make this right with God."

I was stunned. No lecture, no guilt, no condemnation—just the opportunity to be forgiven. I don't remember how long he left us alone, but we were clearly not alone. On our knees, two 17-year-olds who were about to become the object of judgment and gossip at school and church, were asking and accepting the forgiveness of Jesus.

I don't know what was said in the other room, but that night we experienced reconciliation of parents and children, sinners and a Savior. That simple instruction to "Make it right with God" took the shame out of our sin and restored broken hearts. For the first time I understood the gratitude of the woman caught in adultery, the joy of the blind man who could see his Savior's face, and the power of the Word spoken from the cross, "Father forgive them. . . ."

The doctor didn't have to call my parents—they called him. He gave me wonderful care for the next five months and proudly delivered the baby that blessed our lives. The doctor was as happy as our parents when he announced, "It's a girl."

*Ann T. as told to Phyllis Harmony*

# WHEN GOD
## breaks through

Words of judgment easily come to our lips: "That's lame." "What a joke." But when you've seriously blown it, do words of judgment really help? Maybe that's why Ann thought of Jesus' talk with a woman, which is recorded in John 8. Hoping to trap Jesus, the religious leaders of Israel dragged before him a woman caught in the act of adultery. Would he condemn her? Would he ignore what she did? At the end of that story is Jesus' amazing response:

> *Jesus straightened up and asked her, "Woman, where are they? Has no one condemned you?"*
>
> *"No one, sir," she said.*
>
> *"Then neither do I condemn you," Jesus declared.*
> *"Go now and leave your life of sin" (John 8:10–11, NIV).*

His forgiveness gave her the courage to walk away and start a new life.

## my
## CHALLENGE

Feeling condemned? Study the passage above from John 8 and Romans 8:1. Keep reading these words until you really believe them. How would you share this message with someone who feels condemned?

## discovering **GOD** in the details

It had been a bad day. And not just your ordinary bad day when you forget your homework or your hair doesn't look quite right. Even the day I got dressed in the dark and wore mismatched shoes to the bus stop was not this bad.

First I had to work on a beautiful Saturday. That was bad enough, but I overslept and I was late. When I finally ran into the hotel gift shop where I worked and unlocked the front door, a horde of angry travelers rushed in behind me, unhappy that I had made them wait three minutes to make their purchases.

I listened to phone messages, read notes from the previous shift, washed the windows, and checked out the new display of dog figurines which were crowded on a glass shelf. I planned to rearrange the figurines later.

*Maybe the day will get better*, I hoped and halfheartedly prayed. After all God had bigger concerns than my small frustrations. Wars, starvation, abused children—surely God didn't have time to worry about me.

In the back room I sat down to place some merchandise orders my boss had asked me to make. As I studied her list, *crash!* The sound of breaking glass set my heart racing. I hurried to the main floor. Scattered amid a jumbled mess of broken glass shelving were pieces of ceramic dogs—a smashed tail here, a chopped-off ear there. A completely headless cocker spaniel sat in the middle of it all. It would have been funny if I didn't have to clean it all up.

As I swept up the glass and tried to salvage puppy parts, I grumbled about whoever arranged too many heavy dogs on the fragile glass shelf. That person's carelessness caused me extra work and gave me yet another reason to hate this day.

After I cleaned up the dog carnage, I called my boss and gave her the damage report. As I talked on the phone by the cash register, I glanced at the desk behind me in the office. The phone sitting on the desk was smoking! I yelled to my boss, "The phone is on fire!" and ran back to the office.

I grabbed the cord and pulled it out of the wall. At that moment the fire alarm sounded. Some guy from the front desk ran in with a fire extinguisher and doused the entire phone in foam. He looked at me as if to say, "Why would you set the phone on fire?"

Mercifully my shift ended without any more catastrophes. I headed to my car with one goal—go home and get back in bed. My ears were ringing, I had a headache, and it was 147 degrees outside. (OK, it was only 93 degrees, but when you're having a bad day, 93 feels like 147.)

Traffic was heavy because of two big events in the area, and my 25-minute drive would be at least 90 minutes in that jam. So I planned to take a toll road home. I gave myself a mental pat on the back for thinking ahead. Maybe, just maybe, I might salvage this day yet.

As I approached the toll station, I reached for my wallet to find the 50 cents I needed. Then I remembered. I had forgotten to get change at work. Quickly I scrounged through my wallet for hidden change. Nothing. I opened the change compartment in my car. Pennies. By this time I was at the booth. I stopped and scanned the car floor and console. One quarter was all I found.

*How can I not have another quarter?*

One quarter prevented me from taking the fast, traffic-free toll road home. Without that quarter I was condemned to sit in traffic.

"God, can I not have one thing go right today?" I whispered. Tears of frustration filled my eyes.

I looked down and noticed my skirt was partially closed in the door.

*Great, I can't even get in my car without having a problem.* Self-pity filled my heart as I opened the door to pull my skirt back in. And on the ground right next to my car I saw a shiny quarter!

You would have thought I found a million dollars! A quarter was

> **He looked at me as if to say, "Why would you set the phone on fire?"**

exactly what I needed to salvage my day, and a quarter was exactly what God provided.

I quickly tossed my two quarters in the toll basket and sped away.

So I had a bad day. So what? The creator of the universe had met my simplest need in a miraculous way, and I couldn't have been more grateful or more in awe of his love for me.

*Nina Edwards*

# WHEN GOD
## breaks through

Ever have a bad day? Maybe your life feels like one long, bad day right now. Believe it or not, God is at work in your life. As Jesus reminded his disciples: "Look at the ravens. They don't plant or harvest or store food in barns, for God feeds them. And you are far more valuable to him than any birds" (Luke 12:24, NLT). This means he cares about the details of your life—all of them. You are the beloved. Knowing this can give you the strength to face the challenging days when doubts dim your perspective.

## my
# CHALLENGE

List some of the details of your life—things that worry you, decisions you need to make soon, moments that give you joy and purpose. Talk to God about this list, just as you would share details of your life with a friend.

# CUTTING THROUGH THE PAIN 7

## learning how much **GOD** loves you

Sharp, stinging pain. Blood trickling down my arm. A nail file, glistening bright red, had suddenly released all my hurts. I knew I had crossed over to a forbidden place. But the tapes in my head calling me stupid and ugly were silent. At least for now my dull, inner pain was gone—eclipsed by the pain in my body.

Eighth grade can be brutal. I don't know a soul who thinks it was the best time of life. Still there's no comfort in hearing "This will pass" or "Life will get better." How could life get better if I didn't know what was making it bad? How could anything get better if I continued being the person I was?

My family seemed disappointed in me in every way, and I didn't know how I could make myself more acceptable. I wasn't smart like my brother. I wasn't pretty like my mother. I wasn't ambitious or outgoing like my father.

I had no friends, but I didn't know why. I couldn't figure out why I felt like I had the plague or why I was such an easy target for the popular girls to mock. Why couldn't I meet anyone's expectations? Why did I feel like such an outcast? At times I could do nothing more than shut down. Stop feeling. Stop talking. Stop being anything.

That's when I began to cut myself. For a short while physical pain distracted me from the indescribable pain in my heart. Cutting made me feel real again, and I felt a hundred times better after I did it. It worked for me—that's all I knew.

I never let on that I was coping by cutting. I wasn't looking to be found out and I didn't want to die. I was just looking for release. If my parents ever discovered I was a cutter, I was certain it would totally alienate us, and I didn't want that. I just wanted the situation to be different between us and for them to accept me for who I was. But they weren't going to change. I needed someone to talk to, but I didn't have anyone. So for two years, I cut. Cutting became my friend.

Then a girl I knew only a little invited me to go with her on a church retreat. I didn't know anything about God or whether he was even real, but I thought this would be a great chance to get away from my parents and brother for a weekend.

The whole retreat seemed planned just for me. I was amazed how loved I felt. People listened to my situation with my family and my problems at school. They heard how confused and lonely I was. And they prayed for me! I didn't know prayer could be so powerful. I felt God's arms wrap around me and hold me, and I heard his words in my ear: "I love you like no one else ever could. Look to me and I will give you the desires of your heart—I will give you love. I will give you myself."

I wanted to stay in that place forever, but I knew that the weekend had to end. I realized I needed to stay in the church group with these

## Cutting became my friend.

people and keep learning about what love felt like. I needed to learn how real love gets inside a person. I began to realize that I didn't want to escape reality; I wanted to be part of intense reality—God's reality. I would not let others' lies have power over me any longer.

Not long after the retreat, I stumbled onto a Bible passage that hit me hard: "Don't you know that your body is the temple of the Holy Spirit, who lives in you and was given to you by God? You do not belong to yourself, for God bought you with a high price. So you must honor God with your body" (1 Corinthians 6:19–20, NLT). Since it was true that God loved me so much, I needed to be careful with the body he had given me. I needed to get help to stop cutting and find relief in God.

My parents haven't changed since the retreat. They still seem disappointed in me. But I am learning that everyone is sinful and flawed, not just me. We all make mistakes and hurt the people around us. I have decided to pray for my family. Maybe someday they will experience real love too. Meanwhile since I know my friends at church love me and pray for me and don't mind that I am not perfect, I am sticking with them.

*Anonymous*

# WHEN GOD
## breaks through

If you had to write down three things you dislike about yourself, how long would that take? How about three things you like about yourself? Almost none of us will have trouble writing down what we don't like; in fact we might have trouble limiting the list to three things. But when it comes to what we like about ourselves, most of us will struggle to come up with one thing.

Did you know God has a long list of things he likes about you? Why? Because he created you to be precisely who you are! And he loves you just the way he made you. The lies of this world make us doubt God's love for us, but that love is true and real and never changing. As the psalm writer said, "Thank you for making me so wonderfully complex! Your workmanship is marvelous—and how well I know it" (Psalm 139:14, NLT).

## my
## CHALLENGE

Finish this sentence as if you were writing a song to God: "Thank you, God, for making me _____ , _____ , and _____ ."

# THE RAGING FIRE 8

## discovering the **VALUE** of watching your words

The campfire was burning nicely. I was 13 and my first year in our youth group had been a great experience. I was glad the older kids had taken us newbies under their wings. We had a great youth minister too. He was an amazing leader and Christian who seemed to do no wrong. He was fantastic. He—was my dad. Maybe he wasn't all that fantastic and didn't always do everything right, but it was true—everyone loved him.

So here we were camped on this beautiful lake in northwest Arkansas. I was stoking the campfire when Julie, one of my classmates, walked up to me and asked, "Is it true that Barbara is saying bad things about me?"

Apparently another friend of ours told her what was being said by other people—a conversation of the "She said this . . . then he said . . . then so-and-so said" variety.

Now I'm a quiet guy who really doesn't like to create problems and I didn't like some of the games I'd seen girls play with each other. So how was I to answer this? Thoughts raced through my mind. I remembered the conversation when Barbara called Julie a slut. But Barbara was one of the older girls who had helped me out. So what was I to do? How should I answer?

Like any other seventh grade boy, I said nothing. I just looked at Julie.

Julie stepped closer, and with her big brown eyes tearing asked, "Did Barbara call me a slut?"

I thought, *Man, I could be down at the lake skipping rocks. But no! Here I am stoking the fire and getting in hot water.*

I couldn't ignore the question. If I were truthful I'd hurt Julie's feelings and make Barbara angry. If I spared Julie's feelings, I'd be lying. Like a mouse I squeaked, "Well, yeah."

Leave it to me to stoke both fires at the same time. In an instant Julie disappeared into her tent only to reemerge a few minutes later with the friend who had originally shared the information with her.

I began to see people scurry around with purpose, just a few at first, then a few more. Finally the whole camp looked like an ant bed as my friends darted from tent to tent rallying their troops for the showdown.

Barbara must have heard because I saw her gathering her supporters too. The groups marching by grew bigger and bigger.

I looked toward Dad, but he was at the other fire cooking steaks, oblivious to the inferno that was headed his way.

### *Here I am stoking the fire and getting in hot water.*

Thank goodness, Kay, one of our Sunday school teachers, was there. She saw what was happening and intervened, trying to cool down the flames. First she talked with Julie, then with Barbara, then with both of them together. Kay eventually sat everyone down to talk about gossip and words. But the emotional jabs left a battlefield strewn with a variety of wounded.

When Dad realized what had happened, he and Kay discussed the situation and decided she should handle it since the situation involved mostly girls.

And what about me? Well, God was hurting with me. I know this because I was talking to him the whole time.

I've learned to be much more careful with what I say. Dad told me I should watch my words and choose my battles. Not everything needs to be said. I never should have answered Julie's question. Perhaps I should have directed her back to Barbara, or maybe just collapsed and played possum. I know I shouldn't run from my problems, but next time I'm going to skip a few more rocks down at the water's edge and leave the fire to someone else.

*Dennis Stout*

# WHEN GOD
## breaks through

In sports a mouth guard offers protection against a careless elbow or a piece of equipment. Dennis learned the hard way that "he who guards his mouth and his tongue keeps himself from calamity" (Proverbs 21:23, NIV). This is one of many verses in Proverbs on the dangers of unguarded words. But how many times have we failed to grasp that lesson? We open our mouths and *boom!* Someone gets hurt. But like the watchmen of old who stood on city walls observing who entered and exited a city, we are to watch the words that exit our mouths.

## my
## CHALLENGE

What are some ways you guard your words? Why is guarding your words important? What will you do this week to guard your words?

THE WORLD'S WORST DRIVER 9

## learning **GOD'S COMPASSION** through failure

"I can't do it!" 12-year-old Brandon shouted, shoving his papers away. He glared at me as if daring me to challenge him.

We had been struggling to read the simple words on the page—words he needed to learn for the test. He was getting tenser and more nervous with each missed syllable. When I didn't answer he tried another tactic.

"You don't understand, Miss-Goody-Two-Shoes. I always fail these tests. I bet you never failed at anything."

I looked at him, wondering how to respond. This was one of my first real jobs as an assistant tutor at an after-school program, and the kids often didn't take me seriously because I was only 19 and looked like an older sister to them.

I needed something to help this kid. Brandon was angry, insolent, and a terrible reader. His brief struggle to read had left him shaky and rude.

He was right though. I had never had trouble reading and I wondered how to relate. Brandon was looking at the ground fighting tears when suddenly I saw myself just two years earlier fighting a similar battle.

"I have failed," I said quietly. "I used to be the world's worst driver. I failed my driving test five times."

"What?" he said with a smirk. "No way!"

It was true. Like every other 17-year-old, I had been excited about driving. All of my friends had barely studied for the test the night before, had a few driving lessons from their parents, and aced the test.

"No problem, Colleen," they said. "If we aced it, you can too. It was no sweat."

So they were somewhat confounded when I told them I had failed the driving portion of the test.

"You must have had a hard instructor," they consoled me.

They were right. He was a grim little man who looked eager to fail me.

"I just want you to know I rarely pass first-timers," he said with a cold smile that made me break out in a sweat. True to his word, I had barely pulled out of the parking lot when he said, "Turn around. You failed that part."

I don't know what I did wrong, but everything went downhill after that. I began to get nervous and made stupid mistakes, such as forgetting to signal when changing lanes and cutting people off in my panic.

After I failed the test the third time, even my mother got concerned. We were going to move soon, and she really needed me to drive the other car. The pressure was on. And with the added pressure, I got worse instead of better.

The fourth test came, and again I failed. Though I was fine driving on my own, when I got into the car with the driving instructor my brain went numb and I could not think. On test

## "Turn around.

## You have failed."

number five, I was doing fine until the instructor pointed out a mistake. I was waiting at a red light ready to turn right. I knew I was supposed to wait for the traffic to clear, but I panicked and pulled in front of the oncoming car, barely missing it. Needless to say, I failed.

I really wanted to give up. I begged my mom to find someone else to drive, but there was no one else.

"You are just going to have to pass this time," she said sternly. "You are an honor student. Why can't you pass a simple driving test?"

I had no answer. I only knew that nothing seemed to come easily to me. For some reason I was having a major brain block on this whole driving test.

Two weeks before moving, the dreaded final test was upon me. I sat in the car muttering the laws of the road over and over and trying not to hyperventilate. My mouth was as dry as cotton as I prayed for a kind instructor. To my intense relief a cheerful-looking man opened the door and smiled. He glanced at my records.

"Having a hard time with this are you?" he asked sympathetically. I was on the verge of tears and could not answer.

He seemed to understand. "Don't worry. I'll help you pass this time. Just take a deep breath and follow my instructions. Don't panic and keep your eyes on the road."

It was as if God himself had gotten into the car with me. The driving instructor was so kind and reassuring that I relaxed a little. He was *for* me, not against me. I could do it. Before I knew it the test was nearly over. I made minor mistakes, but nothing like the life-threatening ones I had made before. Though I received a low score, I passed.

"You did it!" He laughed as I burst into the tears that had been threatening all day.

"Thank you," I said gratefully. "Thank you for helping me believe in myself."

"No problem. I understand what it's like to have a case of bad nerves."

I remembered this kind man's words as I looked at the belligerent boy before me, who believed he would only fail.

"Don't worry. I am going to help you pass this test," I said with a smile. "If I can fail five times and finally pass, you can too."

He relaxed a little and picked up the paper.

I may have been the world's worst driver, but God used my humiliating experience to help me identify with Brandon. For that, I was glad.

*Colleen J. Yang*

# WHEN GOD
## breaks through

When life is difficult, it's hard to imagine comforting someone else. But Colleen learned what the apostle Paul wrote about in 2 Corinthians. "All praise to the God and Father of our Master, Jesus the Messiah! Father of all mercy! God of all healing counsel! He comes alongside us when we go through hard times, and before you know it, he brings us alongside someone else who is going through hard times so that we can be there for that person just as God was there for us" (2 Corinthians 1:3–4, MSG).

## my
## CHALLENGE

Think about your recent struggles, disappointments, and failures. How did God comfort you in those times? Was it through a Bible verse, a call from a friend? As you consider how you were comforted, think of someone you can comfort.

## experiencing the **JOY** of a debt forgiven

"Sorry, we are closed," the receptionist said. "Come back tomorrow."

I couldn't believe it. It was only 3:50, and the financial aid office was supposed to be open until 4:00.

"Please, just give me a minute!" I cried as the door slammed in my face.

I walked out of the four-story building at the University of Michigan in Ann Arbor and couldn't imagine feeling smaller and with less power. I was 18 years old and all alone.

At 16, I left my home in New York and headed to college. I'd decided to graduate early from high school because I didn't want to be blamed for another divorce.

When I was 11, my father left my mother. He told me he divorced my mother because I needed a new mother. After a few years this new mother proved to be imperfect, and my father was once again threatening to leave.

Although my father had a good job, we had saved no money for my college education. (Divorces are expensive.) For the first two years, I financed school through student loans, income from my work study job as a research assistant in the Department of Psychology, as a nursery school substitute teacher, and with help from my father. But during those two years, every time my father and I had a disagreement, he reminded me of the money he had given me and how much he had sacrificed so I could go to school.

"You owe me," my father said. Those three words became a mantra that made me feel enslaved to him forever. For 16 years I believed them without question.

*You owe me.* I owed him my unconditional loyalty. It was unacceptable to ever say a kind word about my mother.

*You owe me.* When my father needed to vent about his day at work or his marriage, he would cry on my shoulder.

*You owe me.* During my senior year of high school, I had to make sure the house was clean, buy groceries, and put food on the table while my father attended school.

*You owe me.* My body also belonged to him.

At age 18, while spending a semester in Scotland, I began having intense nightmares, anxiety attacks, and flashbacks. I finally admitted aloud that my father had sexually abused me regularly for many years. I could admit this because I was finally far enough away and felt physically safe.

After years of being strong, burying my feelings, and making allowances for any behavior, my emotions caught up with me. I was depressed, and I knew something had to change. Even though I was 600 miles away from my father, the emotional

**I was depressed, and I knew something had to change.**

ties were still powerful. I just couldn't accept another penny from him. Too many suffocating strings were attached. I would apply for financial aid, take out loans if needed, and finish school, returning to my father's house only for visits. Surely I could make it on my own.

That year I was in school taking 19 credits. I worked two jobs—as a personal care assistant for a paraplegic man and at a group home for mentally ill adults. I was sure if I could earn money to buy food and pay rent and other living expenses, I could get aid for my college tuition. I filled out the necessary paperwork, applying for any aid, scholarships, and grants that I could.

One day I received a letter explaining that I didn't qualify for aid. Because my father still claimed me on his income taxes, the government didn't consider me financially independent. How could I stay in school? I couldn't work any more than I was already working. I was completely stressed out, crying constantly, and not sleeping. What more could I do?

I made phone call after phone call, trying to find out about other sources of money: scholarships, other loans, an appeal process. Doors seemed to slam all around me.

At this point I went to the financial aid office and found the door slammed in my face yet again. I walked out of that building, not sure where to go. I just trudged through the snow. After a while I ended up at a small park in a residential neighborhood. I began to pray.

As a small child when I had nightmares that I couldn't share with anyone or when I was a young teen with no one to wipe away my tears, I would pray to God. So that day in the park, I cried out to God. "I don't know where to turn. I have done all I know to do. I surrender."

I continued to pray and cry until I felt like I had no more tears in me and I was ready to collapse. In the bitter cold and quiet of that park, I knew my prayers weren't being offered to deaf ears. The hopelessness in my heart was replaced with a warm feeling that God was with me.

In my early teens I had read Isaiah 49:15 (NIV), which says, "Can a mother forget the baby at her breast and have no compassion on the child she has borne? Though she may forget, I will not forget you!"

This verse was important to me because my mom hadn't fought for custody of me and hadn't protected me. My mom didn't have compassion, but I knew God did. He rescued me from my home and brought me to a safe place. I was reminded that God would always be with me.

On the following day I went back to the financial aid office and talked with a counselor. She listened to my story, and then said she might be able to help me. But she would need time.

Hours later the counselor called me back to the office and asked me how much I still owed in tuition. The figure was well over $4,000.

She sat at her computer and pulled up my records, then called me to her side of the desk. Placing her cursor at the end of the $4,000, she hit the backspace button, slowly erasing my debt. She then told me about a scholarship she had found for me!

"What else do I have to do?" I asked.

"Nothing," she replied. "Your debt has been paid. Just do well this semester."

I left that office not quite sure what had just happened. But I was sure of one thing: God was real. I knew with all certainty that ultimately he had taken away my debt. All my previous efforts at fighting the system, applying for scholarships, and working more had not been enough.

In the park I knew that I had nothing left to do but surrender to God. He alone had the resources to pay my debt.

*Kim Moore*

# WHEN GOD
## breaks through

Jesus told a story about a forgiven debt in Matthew 18:23–35. A servant owed his master money. But the servant couldn't pay back the huge debt—totaling in the millions. So Jesus said, "And out of pity for him, the master of that servant released him and forgave him the debt" (Matthew 18:27, ESV). Although this is a story about forgiveness versus unforgiveness, it also reminds us of God's compassion that covers humongous debts. After all the biggest debt all of us owed—our strong desire to do wrong things—was paid by Jesus' death on the cross. Because God sent his son to cover our debt, we can trust that he'll always help us.

## my
## CHALLENGE

What are your debts? These don't always include money. A debt could be a friend or family member that you haven't forgiven or a task you promised to do that you haven't yet accomplished. Make a list of what you "owe" to your parents, to your family, to your friends, to your teachers. Ask God to help you "pay" those debts—and where it is impossible to do so in your power, ask God to cover your debt for you.

# being **RECONCILED** after rebellion

At my high school in Grand Island, Nebraska, I had a "good girl" image: decent grades, didn't cause trouble, and was raised in the church. But I was attracted to the "bad boys." Something intrigued me about being with a guy who represented everything my family wasn't.

Toward the end of high school, I got involved with my own "bad boy" who was a grade ahead of me. Although he said sweet things to me and genuinely liked me, deep down I knew he wasn't good for me. So I lied to my parents about him. I'd sneak out to see him, telling my mother I was with my best friend, Annie. When my parents found out, naturally they flipped.

I asked myself, *Why can't I just drop this guy?* Then I told myself that he wasn't *that bad* and maybe being around my family would make him want to change. *Yeah, that's it. I'm actually helping him by being with him.*

By the time I graduated, I realized Danny was pulling me away from everything solid: my family, friends, and what little faith I still had. Danny was doing drugs—maybe even selling them—and ran with a crowd I didn't even like. It surprised me how Danny managed to elude jail time. Maybe his not getting caught made it easier for me to prolong breaking off with him. Once again it made sense to excuse him—*he's not that bad, even if he's not that good.*

We were sleeping together and Danny had a strong hold on my heart, but I felt trapped. This wasn't how I was raised and wasn't what I wanted! I wasn't a slut. But I'd become a liar. I lied to my parents and to myself.

By then I also noticed that Danny was controlling and jealous, calling me at all hours, expressing disdain toward my girlfriends. He would tell me to leave wherever I was to go see him or go home. He was suspicious of my platonic male friends—guys I'd grown up with. Although he'd been sweet at the beginning of our relationship, he became condescending and critical of me.

One day the unthinkable happened. I took a home pregnancy test and it was positive. I called my youth leader, Danette, and then went to see her. She'd always encouraged me, even when I stopped attending youth group. I remember a card she once sent me when I was struggling. I had just surrendered my life to Jesus, but still had a hard time saying no to partying. In the card she wrote a verse about the Israelites complaining in the desert and wanting to go back to Egypt where they'd been enslaved. She then wrote, *Rachel, don't go back to Egypt.*

**Rachel, don't go back to Egypt.**

At Danette's house, after small talk about summer vacation, I was ready to talk, but wanted Danette to open the door. She gently said, "I think I can guess what's wrong."

"What?"

"You're pregnant."

I started crying and Danette hugged me. As I sobbed I said, "I always said God would have to let something really big happen to wake me up. I guess this is it!"

Danette reassured me that this news wasn't bigger than God. She held my hand as I called my mom to tell her the news. That was a painful phone call to make because I had a good relationship with my mom.

That conversation was almost as painful as the look on my father's face when I told him. My parents were honest about their disappointment with me and their anger toward Danny. Though they were more committed to me than ever, my entire family was hurt.

You can't predict how your choices will affect others. My sister, who'd just gotten engaged and set a wedding date, postponed her wedding because it was around my due date. She loves me dearly, but this hindered her, her fiancé, and the rest of her wedding party.

Still my family didn't treat me as if I'd ruined life for them. They didn't make excuses for me. Instead, they allowed me to move past shame and regret to a fresh spiritual and literal reboot.

Regaining a sense of self-respect didn't happen overnight. I had long talks with my parents and youth leader to help me set healthy boundaries with Danny. I had to work to keep my head clear when my baby's father talked down to me or tried to pressure me into sex after that.

My pregnancy was one of the most difficult times of my life. Though I wanted Danny to be a part of our baby's life, everything came to a thundering wreck one week when he almost became physically violent. I finally had the courage to end our relationship.

The greatest hero in all this was Jesus. He knew when I first began making those secret choices to deceive my parents and myself. He knew when I chose a guy's affection over his unwavering love. He remained a committed, faithful Savior. Spending time with him took me beyond "survival" mode. He gave me hope for my future again.

A year after my baby's birth, my best friend Annie became pregnant while unmarried. With the help of another youth leader, I started a new mom's Bible study at church. I lived at home and worked to save money for the next chapter. It wasn't easy, but life wasn't over.

*Rachel P. as told to Danette Matty*

## WHEN GOD
### breaks through

Rachel had the courage to continue, even when life was hard. She discovered a truth vividly described by the Old Testament prophet Isaiah: "'Come now, let us reason together,' says the LORD. 'Though your sins are like scarlet, they shall be as white as snow; though they are red as crimson, they shall be like wool'" (Isaiah 1:18, NIV). These words were spoken to God's rebellious people, Israel. God is also willing to forgive and forget, even when we blow it. Forgiveness doesn't mean we're exempt from the consequences of our actions, but it does give us a fresh start.

### my
### CHALLENGE

Do you need a fresh start? Do you have the courage to grab your journal and write down how you think you've blown it? Afterward talk to God about it, then take your pen or pencil and mark out what you just wrote. His forgiveness removes your wrong.

## coping with a **DIFFICULT** relationship

I attended church with my grandparents from the time I was very small, but I acted like my peers who slept in on Sunday mornings. I had a horrible relationship with my stepdad and the bitterness about that colored everything I did.

My mother and stepdad married and divorced four times while I was growing up. Even though I could have lived by myself during the last two years of high school, I stayed with them to protect my mother from my stepfather's domineering behavior.

My stepdad tried to control me too. For instance he insisted that I ask permission for a drink of water or food when my mother was at work. When I didn't, he screamed at me and made me spit out whatever was in my mouth until I asked his permission. I refused to ask. I only ate when my mom provided it, which was about one meal a day.

I was an awkward girl with boyish tendencies—unlike my beautiful, petite mom—and my stepdad threatened to send me away to a finishing school. He found fault with everything I did and was.

When I was 16, I attended a church youth convention where I decided to follow Christ. I thought this decision would somehow change my life overnight—God would change my situation at home and I would automatically clean up my act and stop living like my unsaved friends. I came to understand that God would not change my situation immediately, but he gave me a new assurance that he would protect me.

Then my family moved. Without the support of my former church and relationships, I developed a sarcastic, negative attitude and felt angry with my mom for staying with my stepdad. I started at my new school that fall not connected with any Christians.

The pain continued. My stepdad accused me of being promiscuous even though I wasn't. He showed up after school to see if I walked out of the doors with any kids he disapproved of. He talked about "hearing" things from teachers or coaches about people I was talking to at school, even if it was a normal interaction in the hallway. His accusations began to change the way I looked at myself.

Over the next year I destroyed my reputation by being shamelessly flirtatious and cursing like a sailor. I didn't participate fully in school, though I desperately longed to be part of a group—any group. I had no real friends and I tried to hide who I really was from people at church and from my mom. I only kept going to church because it was a chance to get away from my stepdad.

Toward the end of my senior year, my pastor announced that the church was holding a baptism service. After church the pastor said that because I had given my life to Jesus when I was 16, he thought I should be baptized. I figured I must be OK if my pastor thought I was and I agreed to do it. I remember panicking, though, because I **His accusations began to change the way I looked at myself.** thought baptism was something you did after you had everything together, and I knew I was far from perfect. But I went to a couple of classes at the church that taught about baptism. Surprisingly, no one pointed a finger at me about my life. I continued to think maybe I was acceptable even though my lifestyle was not what it was supposed to be.

The day of the baptism I sat in the front row waiting nervously. I can't remember what the pastor preached about or any of the songs the people sang, but I remember the voice I heard so clearly. I can only say that it was God, because it was so clear and gentle, and only I heard it. I sensed him telling me that I was OK, and even if people around me couldn't see that, he could. I understood that God wanted to make my life worth something. If I would completely give myself to him, God would help me with everything.

I went right up to the altar and poured out my heart to him. I told him I was sorry for my sins and asked him to be my everything—whatever I needed.

My relationship with my stepdad is still difficult, even though I've left home to attend college. But my relationship with God has helped me give more appropriate and measured responses. I continually pray for God to help me show his love regardless of the situation.

*Faith R. as told to Julie Grimes*

# WHEN GOD
## breaks through

Sometimes a bad situation emphasizes our need for God. Faith's hard relationship with her stepfather caused her to seek assurance from God—the heavenly Father who would never change. Like David the psalmist, she could proclaim: "I trust you, O LORD; I say, 'You are my God'" (Psalm 31:14, NIV). This simple truth can be life-changing. It's not just a declaration of faith, it's also a lifestyle.

## my
## CHALLENGE

What does your trust in God look like? Would others make the above declaration from Psalm 31:14 about you, based on your actions?

# A DRIVE TO REMEMBER 13

## obeying **GOD'S** principles

"Dad! If you let everyone in, we'll never get to school on time."

Unmoved by my outburst and other drivers honking, Dad just smiled and waved another merging driver ahead. Turning to me he said, "Son, I am trying to walk the Word."

Walk the Word. I rolled my eyes. A fresh layer of snow made the roads more dangerous than normal, and we were driving during morning rush hour. How could *that* be a spiritual experience?

"Why do you have to make everything religious? I don't see a spiritual lesson here, Dad. I just want to get to school."

Since I'm a preacher's kid, I should have known better than to push him, but sometimes I get fed up and just want to be a normal teen. Stealing a look at his face, I settled into my seat sensing a minisermon coming. It was going to be a long ride to school.

Carefully navigating our old sedan into the turn lane for Highway 41, Dad said, "Mike, during my quiet time this morning, I read God's promise in Joshua: 'I will never leave you' (Joshua 1:5, 9). It occurred to me that the flipside is more often the case."

And then he paused.

Being a preacher, Dad knows just how and when to deliver a pregnant pause. Mentally counting the bumps in the road as the tires hit the lane markers, I imagined how great it would be when I could drive myself to school. I wondered what my life would be if my parents were regular people who liked to cheer a rousing Vikings game on Sunday instead of preferring after-church fellowship over a chicken casserole and weak coffee.

"God doesn't leave us, but we leave him—every day in so many ways."

"For example," he continued, "being in the push-and-shove of rush hour traffic. I can't let others' harsh words and manic behaviors affect me. How can I walk away from spending time in thanks for the day God has for me, and then turn into a raging lunatic who obsesses over other people's driving habits?

"I'm driving in a different race, Mike, the race for life, and I aim to win. If I forget my convictions and act like the angry drivers, I lay aside any peace I gained during my morning prayer. Worse, I dishonor Jesus."

Dishonor Jesus. He had to toss that phrase in. It's not enough to resist the push and pull of peer pressure, drugs, and premarital sex. Who wants to add another heavy load to the mix? With everything a guy's got against him in the world, at least you need God on your side.

Glancing out the window I saw a red-faced man flinging his finger our way. In that moment I realized what a senseless act it is, and how stupid to react to it. Laughing to myself I started to see Dad's point. I faced Dad, thankful he has always been there to set the course.

**I wondered what my life would be if my parents were regular people who liked to cheer a rousing Vikings game on Sunday.**

"I suppose that's what happens to me in school," I said. "I know I shouldn't dishonor Jesus, especially when I try to live a life I think Jesus would be proud of. But when everyone is making fun or hassling me, I get so frustrated I want to punch out a locker!"

"Son, I know just what you mean. Kind of makes you wonder if what we gain in acting out is worth what we lose, doesn't it?" he asked as he exited onto Pioneer Trail. "It can be a struggle sometimes to keep the grace of the morning in the grit of the day, but I believe it's worth it. Let Jesus walk with you through your day."

As we pulled into the Chaska High parking lot, I gathered my books and zipped my coat. But before I jumped out of the car, Dad had a last word: "I'll pray for you today, Mike."

I stopped and looked around. I figured few, if any of the others heading into school heard those words that morning. It's not so bad having a father who really cares, one who recognizes my desires, good and bad, and yet pushes me to a higher ground.

"I know you will, Dad. That's what makes it all right." I rushed the words as my feet hit the pavement and I slammed the door, ready to run for the school.

"Love you, Son." Actually, I didn't hear him say that, but I felt it. Squaring my shoulders with the knowledge that both Jesus and Dad walked with me, I smiled and seized the day.

*Mike B. as told to Tama Joy Westman*

## WHEN GOD
### breaks through

Mike's dad realized what the Old Testament king of Israel, David, knew: the value of honoring God by obeying him. This is why David could write from the heart:

"*Teach me your decrees, O LORD; I will keep them to the end. Give me understanding and I will obey your instructions; I will put them into practice with all my heart. Make me walk along the path of your commands, for that is where my happiness is found*" (Psalm 119:33–35, NLT).

### my
## CHALLENGE

What pressures are pulling you away from God rather than toward him today? Make a list. Then pray using David's words from Psalm 119—ask God to give you understanding and the strength to obey his instructions. Tell God how you plan to put his instructions into practice.

## moving beyond the **HEARTTHROB** to true love

Eric was tall, dark, extremely good-looking (raven black hair and brown eyes), and the bane of my life.

The guy had no clue what he did to girls like me. He seemed wholly unaware of his good looks and yet he was moody—at times friendly and responsive and other times indifferent. This combination made him intriguing, but also infuriating.

I first noticed him at church when we were both in middle school. He was the quiet, shy boy who, like me, hung around the fringes at church social events. I tried to talk to him, but got little response.

A few years later we still belonged to the same youth group but attended different high schools. Still we developed a friendship.

I studied him as thoroughly as I studied for my history test. I knew his hobbies, what he liked to eat, and what he liked to wear. I even studied his favorite bands so I could have something to talk to him about.

Little by little he began to trust me and tell me his problems. I was there for him when no one else was. When he sent out an invitation to a fashion show for aspiring young models that he was part of, I was his only friend to show up. When he wanted to go to an underground dance club, I dressed my craziest. I told myself I was happy to just be his friend.

By this time Eric had shot up in height, filled out, and become a hot item. Karen was one of those girls who wanted him, but only as part of her collection. With her big brown eyes and lithe, tan figure, she easily had a dozen guys interested in her.

Another blond beauty named Michelle broke Eric's heart when she didn't show up after promising him she would meet him at a skating party. I tried to comfort him, hoping he would notice that I was there to fill in. But he never did. To him I was just an old friend, not a romantic possibility.

I was infuriated with girls like Michelle and Karen who had a feminine draw, but used it to toy with guys' hearts, feed their egos, and then later toss them aside.

That wouldn't be me, I determined. I had earned Eric's friendship. I would now show him that truth was better than popularity, and he would realize that he had loved me all along. But I was only deceiving myself and getting hurt in the process.

It was amazing what I put up with. A group of us were hanging out in the back of the church. Karen and I stood on some benches with some of the guys standing below. Looking coy, Karen shouted, "Catch me!" and jumped into Eric's arms.

Since I was standing there too, she said slyly, "Come on, jump! Eric will catch you. Right, Eric?"

"Uh, yeah," he said laughing. "Go ahead and jump."

**I was only deceiving myself and getting hurt in the process.**

Like a dope I fell for it. I jumped, he moved, and I fell, scraping my knees while the others laughed.

The sting of my knees was nothing compared to the sting of betrayal. Humiliated, I determined that I would no longer be the idiot. I was through with Eric! But then he would call or smile at me and I would follow him again, trying to care for him unconditionally and feeling more alone after being with him. It was like living in a desert.

Finally the summer after high school, I moved into a dorm room at Biola Christian College in La Mirada, California. Few people had arrived on campus yet, but I found plenty of opportunities to hear people speak about God. I had experienced brief episodes of spirituality at summer camps, but had never lived surrounded by people who loved God and wanted to know him. It was like water to my dry and needy heart.

One day a chapel speaker talked about how we need God to fill our cup—that only he can love us the way we need to be loved. If we look for love in other places, he said, it will only be like drinking out of a broken cup. That kind of "love" may satisfy for a while, but the water will soon leak out leaving us emptier than before.

Like a bolt of lightning, I realized Eric was like that to me—an empty cup I had been pouring water into, water that leaked away before I could drink any, leaving me thirstier than ever.

*Lord, I want to know what true love is,* I prayed as I returned to my dorm room.

"You will," a voice in my heart said. "But you need to let Eric go."

That was hard at first. When I saw him at church, my heart leapt, but I decided not to hang out with him anymore. As the months passed and I read the Bible and prayed regularly, I learned to find joy in spiritual things and found I didn't need Eric. True love began to fill my emptiness as I learned to love God.

One spring morning I was startled to see my friend Sam waiting for me after class.

"Hi," he said. "Can I walk you home?" His eyes sparkled in a way I hadn't noticed before.

"Sure." I beamed. The desert had begun to bloom.

*C. J. Sylraen*

## WHEN GOD
### breaks through

Ever feel so emotionally invested in a relationship that you're not sure you could ever let it go? Some relationships are toxic. C. J. discovered a relationship she didn't have to release, one that encouraged, instead of discouraged. Like the writer of Psalm 107, she found true love—with God. A passage from that psalm proclaims, "Let them give thanks to the LORD for his unfailing love and his wonderful deeds for men. . . . He turned the desert into pools of water and the parched ground into flowing springs" (Psalm 107:31, 35, NIV).

### my
## CHALLENGE

Time for a reality check. Are you hanging on to any relationships that you know in your heart you need to release? Do you have the courage to get feedback from a trusted friend or family member about these relationships?

# AN ATTITUDE ADJUSTMENT 15

## admitting a **NEED** to change

"I'm not going!" I yelled at my mom as I sunk into the kitchen chair.

Hardly moving from her sandwich-making position, she fired right back, "You're going and that's all there is to it. Now get upstairs and pack."

"Ugh!" I grunted under my breath, instantly regretting it.

"Excuse me?" My mom strangled a piece of lettuce. "Your father and I are paying for your college education. We put the clothes on your back and the food in your stomach. Until you can support yourself and are no longer dependent on us, you will do as you are told!"

This was a lecture I had heard far too many times recently. I stomped up the stairs, suitcase dragging behind me.

The last thing I wanted to do this final week of summer vacation was spend it on the beach with 21 members of my extended family. I love my grandparents, and my aunts and uncles are hilarious, but the idea of sleeping in the same bedroom with eight of my cousins who hadn't hit puberty was not my idea of a good time.

I was soon sitting in the back of a hot, smelly, 15-passenger van, headed toward the coast. Defiantly I began making a mental list of what I would do on this vacation: pout in the corner, devour all the desserts before anyone else could indulge, hide my sister's bathing suit bottom. . . .

I'd been angry about everything all summer long. I tried to blame my resentment on the idea that my heart was still mending from several relationships gone sour. I also convinced myself that the transition during my family's recent cross-country move was getting to me. But deep down I knew I had adopted the attitude of believing everything should go the way I wanted. I was not fun to be around.

After a few miserable hours in the van, we pulled in front of the rented cabin. In spite of every stubborn bone in my body, I knew this vacation would not be as terrible as I had imagined. The cabin was on a beautiful piece of lakefront property on the east side of Puget Sound, outside of Seattle. Dropping my bags in the front entrance, I headed for the backyard beach.

The saltwater left a sweet fragrance in the air as a flock of seagulls squawked. Snowcapped mountains lay in the distance, and the setting sun left a rosy tint on the lake's glassy surface. I sat on the rocky beach near the water's edge and dipped my toes into the lapping waves. Numbness shot through my legs, causing goose bumps. This water was probably refreshing in the afternoon, but at sunset it was too cold to even splash my toes in.

As dusk turned to darkness, I felt God was going to teach me something incredible this week. I just didn't know what.

The week began as chaotic and crazy as could be. My mom's intricate schedule of events filled our days with fun. She made sure I participated in all the events. I took my small cousins to the pool, we kayaked around the water's shore, and we hiked through the lush forest beyond the cabin. In the evening we laughed

**I felt God was going to teach me something incredible this week. I just didn't know what.**

through games of Mexican train dominoes and stuffed our faces. Best of all were the long discussions on the porch as my relatives told how God had been faithful to them even when they found it hard to trust him.

Aunt Paula recalled the years of singleness, before God faithfully brought her a husband beyond her imagination. Uncle Dave told stories from his days of unemployment, when he could barely make ends meet. God led him to a job better than he could have hoped for. I even told about the anonymous donor who helped pay my college tuition.

These conversations caused me to think hard. Why was I so bitter? Why couldn't I trust God with my future? Why was I being so selfish?

One night, near the end of our stay, I sat on the rocky shore. My dad followed me to this resting place and squatted beside me, his arm around my slender shoulders.

"What has God taught you this week?" he asked—his trademark question.

"A lot." The words barely escaped from my lips. Tears filled my eyes, trickled down my cheeks, and caught at the bottom of my chin. Using the cuff of my oversized sweatshirt, I wiped them away and faced my dad. "I have been so selfish, Dad. Not only when I was resentful about coming here, but in most areas of my life. I want that to change. I want to be open to following the desires God has for my life and live for him, not for me." With a sudden impulse I added, "I'd like to be baptized here, with the family as my witnesses, because I know they will always hold me accountable to these new desires of my heart."

Tears brimmed in his eyes as he gave me a giant squeeze that told me how proud he was of my decision.

The next evening, as the sun set, I went to the water's edge again, this time followed by all my family members who were as excited as I was to be baptized at this special reunion.

My dad, the selected pastor, stood waist deep in the clear water, his dark reflection quivering as he called me to join him. The water was just as cold as it had been the first night I tiptoed in.

After a few moments of hesitation, I plunged in, the water numbing my body, and I slowly splashed toward my dad. I squeezed my arms together in hopes of salvaging some of the warmth remaining on my body.

I told everyone about the revelations I learned during this vacation and asked them to keep me accountable as I tried to live fully devoted to the Lord.

My dad said, "I have prayed ever since my girls were born that they would make their own decisions to follow God. This is a moment—not only as Allison's pastor, but as her father—that I have prayerfully waited for."

After a few moments of prayer and meditation, my dad stabilized one arm under my back and plugged my nose with his other hand. In a quick motion he lowered me beneath the shimmering water and brought me back up to my feet. Now colder than ever I ran to my mom who swaddled me in a warm towel and pushed me toward the cabin. I knew from that day forward, my life would never be the same.

Just as quickly as the baptism had occurred, our vacation was over. The following morning we packed up, ready to go home to our fast-paced lives. One last time I went to the beach and stared at the dancing water, reflecting on the past week—the ugly person I'd been upon arrival and the person I was now. Going back home, to the places and people who were still the same, would be difficult. But my baptism was my solid reminder that I was different now. Only through the Lord's help would I be able to get through the tough times in my life.

*Allison Asimakoupoulos*

# WHEN GOD
## breaks through

A first-century jailer in the port city of Philippi had the same request that Allison had—to be baptized. You can read that story in Acts 16:16–40. Baptism is the symbol of a new life. In his letter to the Romans, the apostle Paul said this about baptism: "When we went under the water, we left the old country of sin behind; when we came up out of the water, we entered into the new country of grace—a new life in a new land! That's what baptism into the life of Jesus means" (Romans 6:3, MSG).

## my
## CHALLENGE

Take a moment to honestly evaluate any bad attitudes you've noticed in recent weeks. In what ways do you show a desire to change?

## celebrating a **RESTORED** life

David was eight years old and had been left by the side of the road to die—by his parents!

David was malnourished. Since his parents knew he was dying, they decided to leave him and use their meager food supplies to try to keep other children alive. Sadly they had carried him, as they had done with three other children, to the side of the main road and left him there. When the officials came by they would know to remove the body. But before the officials arrived, our team passed by David.

When I was a high school sophomore in the United States, I was invited to go to Bolivia to work for two weeks with a group of doctors, nurses, and dentists to provide medical and dental care to poor people. I was excited about the chance to miss school for a week, but since we were leaving December 27, I was disappointed that I wouldn't be home to spend New Year's Eve with my friends.

**I was in the Bolivian jungle with a little boy who had literally been brought back from the dead.**

After a long plane flight and riding in the back of a truck up and down and around crazy mountain curves for eight hours, we arrived at a village, set up a little clinic in an abandoned shack, and got to work.

People came from miles around with infections, decayed teeth, and sick children. I worked in the pharmacy, finding and dispensing the medicine prescribed by doctors. I got to say "*Tome dos pildores, tres veces al dia, para diez dias*" (two pills, three times a day, for ten days) more times than I could count.

On December 30 our team split into two groups and went into even more remote areas to work. My team returned first. The other got back late and finally showed up with an extra passenger named David.

David's parents had given them permission to treat David, so the doctors started an IV and began a rotation to monitor him.

The next day was December 31, New Year's Eve Day. David was much more stable, so the doctors let some of us take shifts with him. We fed him broth through an eyedropper and blew bubbles over his head for him to watch. He was amazed by the bubbles and watched them for hours.

I got the midnight shift on New Year's Eve. So instead of celebrating back home with my friends as the new year rolled in, I was in the Bolivian jungle with a little boy who had literally been brought back from the dead. Feeding David with the eyedropper, I heard God tell me to use my own life to give life to those who have been left for dead, physically or spiritually.

It was a new year, and I hadn't partied or counted down the minutes, but I kissed David's dear, dark forehead and thanked God for life regiven.

*Heather Pleier*

# WHEN GOD
## breaks through

In spending her New Year's Eve with a little boy who had been left for dead, Heather discovered the meaning behind Jesus' words to his followers: "If you try to keep your life for yourself, you will lose it. But if you give up your life for my sake and for the sake of the Good News, you will find true life" (Mark 8:35, NLT). When we stop focusing on ourselves and put others' needs ahead of ours, we will find true meaning, purpose, and satisfaction in our lives. That means following where Jesus will lead us instead of chasing our own goals. That may sound hard to do, but when we realize that God knows what real life's all about, it makes good sense.

## my
## CHALLENGE

Write down the goals you have for the next five years, then offer your goals to God in prayer. Ask him to lead you, and ask God to give you the wisdom and strength to follow *his* plans, not your own.

## exploring the reality of **GOD'S** presence

"Great! It's raining!" I muttered angrily. My mother had forgotten to pick me up from school again!

It was late on a cold fall afternoon in Wisconsin. Although fall colors are beautiful, the rainy days can be depressingly dreary and icy cold. I had three miles to walk before I reached home. I had been expecting a ride home from football practice as usual, so I hadn't dressed to face the weather. The wind was whipping and the rain pelted my face. With freezing ungloved hands, I slowly plodded forward, supporting my books under my sweater, keeping my head down and squinting to see where the sidewalk ended and the cross street began. To kill time, I mulled over the choice words I would share with my mother when I finally reached home.

*Why am I always the one she forgets? Out of five kids, why am I expected to do stuff that nobody else is expected to do, like walk three miles in the rain? My sister gets away with everything. She gets a whim to do something and mom's always on board, right there, carting her everywhere she wants to go.*

I had a list in my head of all the activities my sister, Jessica, started but never finished. She even dragged me to a teen Bible study at a friend's church months ago. She didn't want to go alone because she was interested in a guy there, but didn't want to get caught if things got too weird.

Jessica ended up going only that one time, but I stuck with it every week. I had to find my own way to the meetings after that first time, but I guess I hadn't minded. It's true that I kept going because there was a really pretty girl in charge of the meetings, but at least I wasn't a quitter.

After a few weeks, I found that the study discussions were not only fun but also interesting. I was learning about things I had never heard before. Not coming from a church-going family, I didn't know very much about Christianity. I knew about some rituals, but not much about Jesus. This teen group had some really good teachers who showed us all kinds of fascinating verses in the Bible.

**I realized that Jesus was a person rather than a religion.**

At first I was embarrassed that I didn't know anything about finding my way around the Bible. Once I got a feel for it I read passages that really made me curious, and truthfully, also made me feel kind of self-conscious. As I learned about the character of God, the love of God, and some of the promises God had made, I realized that Jesus was a person rather than a religion. Unlike my other studies about world religions, the Jesus of Christianity had already done so much for me before I had even done anything for him. I figured if all this were true about Jesus, then I needed to respond somehow and get more serious about being a Christian.

All these thoughts and memories ran through my rain-soaked head as I trudged past the gas station where I used to regularly fill my bicycle tires with air. I had been avoiding that particular gas station because it was owned by two guys who were so outspoken about Jesus that they made me uncomfortable. Within a few seconds of my riding up, one of the brothers would run up to me and say, "Are you saved? Jesus loves you and has a plan for your life!" I figured they were a little nuts, so I usually went out of my way to get air for my tires someplace else.

But on this dark and dreary day, I wondered if their enthusiasm *wasn't* warranted. After thinking it through, it only made sense for these guys to be outspoken about something so important. I mean if everything I was learning at Bible study was true, then they were right to be so enthusiastic.

The rain slowed to a drizzle. It felt almost warm and inviting in a way. As I stopped trying to dodge raindrops through the tree-lined park and watched the ripples on the pond, I looked up and spoke aloud: "If what I've heard about you is true, then I'm in. I want more of you."

At that moment I realized that I didn't really know how to pray and I didn't know many facts about Jesus. Could I be a Christian even though I hardly knew anything about God? Was I doing it right? Something deep inside me told me not to listen to those questions. What came to my mind instead was something Jesus said: "God blesses those whose hearts are pure, for they will see God" (Matthew 5:8, NLT).

I thought, *That's what I want. I want to see God.* I knew then that I had to respond to what God was telling me in that moment.

I turned my head toward the rain and thought, *This is my baptism—just you and me, God. I trust that you'll take me wherever I am supposed to go and teach me what I need to know.*

During those moments it seemed as though there was no one in the world except God and me. Sounds were muffled and the park was still. The rain was exhilarating, as if God was actually touching me. I stopped hurrying and just enjoyed the feeling of being right where I was meant to be—in the rain, alone with God, just being who I was.

When I reached home, I wasn't mad at my mother. In the days that followed, I stopped avoiding the guys at the gas station. In fact I would make a point of going to their station and talking to them about God. I started attending a Bible study for teenagers and college students. My family and friends noticed how excited I'd become about my faith. I found myself actually looking forward to times when I could walk home, because I could spend it talking with God.

*Ryan S. as told to Gloria Spielman*

## WHEN GOD
### breaks through

The verse Ryan quoted is Matthew 5:8 (NLT): "God blesses those whose hearts are pure, for they will see God." But during a rainstorm, Ryan also learned an ancient truth God spoke through Moses: "Let my teaching fall on you like rain; let my speech settle like dew. Let my words fall like rain on tender grass, like gentle showers on young plants" (Deuteronomy 32:2, NLT). The fact is that those who truly want to know God will definitely find him. Just as a dry plant welcomes water, the spiritually thirsty person welcomes the "rain" of God's words. That's what Ryan did. How about you?

### my
## CHALLENGE

In what ways has the truth of God "fallen" upon you recently? Maybe a friend or family member shared a Bible verse with you or told you that he or she is praying for you. What actions or thoughts did these words encourage within you?

# A CHANGE OF DIRECTION 18

## going **BEYOND** life's impasses

I sat in my new boss's office too stunned to speak. Being program manager of the summer camp I had attended since third grade was the job of my dreams. Camp life suited me perfectly. I'd also been a counselor at the camp and hoped eventually to work my way up to camp director. But now the new camp director was telling me to leave.

"I can either fire you," he said, "or you can resign."

I remained speechless.

"You shouldn't have left camp today," he continued. "We needed you here."

Some counselors and I had taken the campers on a trail ride off the camp grounds. Firing me because I had started a bicycling program seemed like a flimsy reason.

"I thought everybody was OK with me leaving," I said. "Why didn't you tell me before?"

The camp manager spent the next half hour telling me that leaving had not been OK. Then he left me alone in his office.

I stormed from the building and into the darkness, down to the fire pit where for so many years I had sung, prayed, taken part in devotions, and roasted hot dogs and s'mores. Tonight I cried. I loved this camp and now it was rejecting me.

"Why is this happening?" I called out to God. The only answer I heard was my own sobs. Where was God?

A couple of days later, I felt even lower spiritually and emotionally. I applied at other camps, but it was already July. None had openings this far into the summer. Anger and frustration kept building inside, pushing me to take some sort of action.

I headed from home on one of my bicycles. I had no idea where I was going; I just kept pounding the pedals. I soon ended up on a country road surrounded by test fields for seed companies. I saw storm clouds ahead, but I didn't care. I headed north, trying to understand why the new camp manager had fired me. I kept praying, *Why God? What now?* As I kept riding, a large landfill—literally a mountain of trash—came into view. I continued toward it.

The road I was on soon turned into gravel. The tires on my road bike were only an inch wide and not meant for such a surface. I needed to stay on pavement and had to change course. I turned west.

Immediately the horizon changed. The sun bathed the sky in pinks and purples. A rainbow arched across the sky, emerging out of the blackness to the south. I was awestruck by the beauty. I felt God's presence, amazed that he would display such majesty just when I needed a reminder of his power. I kept looking from the darkness in the south to the beauty in the west.

**I headed north, trying to understand why the new camp manager had fired me.**

I came to the end of the westward road and had to change direction again. The skies ahead of me now were even clearer, with bright, puffy clouds. I saw no signs of any storm. That was behind me, like the bad experience at camp. I knew I didn't need to worry anymore.

I kept going, assured that just as God guided me on my bicycle, he would direct my path in life. He had written a promise to me across the sky, a rainbow like the one he gave Noah.

A couple of months later, one of the camps I'd applied to hired me as a program manager.

This incident showed me that even when my future appears bleak, God has a plan for me. I've learned God is always with us, backing us even when the road ahead looks dark.

*Derek B. as told to Ronica Stromberg*

## WHEN GOD
### breaks through

While Derek was focused on his failure and being fired, God gave him a sign of his presence and a new path to follow. If, like Derek, you're reeling from a failure, consider a message God gave the Israelites through the prophet Isaiah: "Forget the former things; do not dwell on the past. See, I am doing a new thing! Now it springs up; do you not perceive it? I am making a way in the desert and streams in the wasteland" (Isaiah 43:18–19, NIV). Through this message, God assured his people that he could create a path even when it looked like they faced a dead end.

### my
## CHALLENGE

Derek prayed about what to do. But he also acted. That's the advice of Proverbs 3:5–6: "Trust in the Lord with all your heart and lean not on your own understanding; in all your ways acknowledge him, and he will make your paths straight" (NIV). Meditate on this passage. Then pray about your options. Are you willing to take the path God chooses?

## sharing one **ANOTHER'S** burdens

I always thought the Bible story about Lazarus' death was really strange, especially the verse that said, "Jesus wept."

Jesus knew he would bring the guy back from the dead. So I never understood why—when he stood outside the tomb and everyone was crying and feeling helpless and desperate—Jesus cried too. He knew he had the power to make the situation right and he knew he was going to raise his friend Lazarus up out of the grave, alive and well.

So this always puzzled me until I met Erma.

My friend Erma loved horses and trained them on her grandma's ranch for years. I like animals too, and they like me. But I don't think I would ever say I loved a horse. Erma, however, loved her horses and never hesitated to say so. And her horses loved her. On the night before a big show, she spent hours combing out the horses' manes and brushing their coats until they shone, getting them ready to trot out into the arena where she would proudly display their talents. She'd put those horses through their paces, and you could see that the animals not only obeyed, but also adored her.

Erma especially loved her newest stallion, Prince Albert. He was just 20 months old when she got him and by age three he was a rising star in the show circles.

Then Prince Albert sprained his hind leg and hobbled in pain for weeks. Despite good care, the leg got worse. Veterinarians tried to figure out what to do; expensive treatments failed. Prince Albert's trotting days were over; even walking hurt him.

I was there when the vet gave the family the bad news: unless they were willing to spend thousands of dollars—much more than they had paid for the horse—nothing could be done for Prince Albert except to put him down.

Erma cried and cried, but she knew her family really didn't have another choice. The doctor pulled out a huge hypodermic needle, filled the syringe with yellow liquid, and gave Prince Albert the lethal shot in the hip. A few minutes later the fine horse lay down, groaning softly and looking at Erma as if he was trying to understand why he suddenly felt so tired. Erma put her arms around his neck and lay down gingerly on his shoulder. She stayed there as his breath grew quieter.

**Nothing could be done for Prince Albert except to put him down.**

Finally he was gone.

And then Erma really let go of her feelings, sobbing inconsolably at the loss of this wonderful horse she loved.

I suddenly realized that I was crying hard too. For a moment that surprised me; I had only known this horse for a couple of months. I wasn't nearly as attached to him as Erma was.

Then it hit me: I wasn't crying because of how I felt about Prince Albert. I was crying because I identified with my friend's feelings about her horse's death. That's when I finally understood why Jesus wept.

*Harold S. as told to Gene Smillie*

# WHEN GOD
## breaks through

Two words, *Jesus wept* (John 11:35, NLT), pack so much meaning. In those two words we see Jesus' humanness. We know he understands when we are in pain. We know he can relate to our weaknesses and our struggles. And not only does he understand what we're going through, he shares in our struggles. We can take comfort because we know Jesus has experienced everything we will ever face. Because he knows what we're going through, he can meet all of our needs in those situations. As the author of Hebrews wrote, "We don't have a priest who is out of touch with our reality. He's been through weakness and testing, experienced it all—all but the sin. So let's walk right up to him and get what he is so ready to give. Take the mercy, accept the help" (Hebrews 4:15–16, MSG).

Don't think for a minute that you have to put on a good front for God. He knows. He's been there. And he's ready to help.

## my
## CHALLENGE

The wonderful thing about experiencing Jesus' compassion and comfort is that we can pass it on to others. Who do you know who is going through a tough time? Who needs the company and encouragement of a friend? Maybe that person is sitting at your lunch table or next to you in class. Ask God to show you how you can help others through their struggles.

# finding my **PATH** in the road of pain

"What on earth are you doing?" Mom asked, laughing.

I suppose it was a valid question. I was running around the living room, throwing matching sheets over threadbare furniture and rearranging pictures. I only knew that George was coming over—the guy who looked like a dream and lived in a fairy-tale house.

Until now I had only known him as my friend Helen's gorgeous 16-year-old brother. When he asked me to go to the spring dance at his high school, I was floored.

His parents were respectable, soft-spoken people who doted on their three kids. They had just moved to a beautiful new upper-class home with white plush carpet and matching furniture. I was embarrassed to have him come to my small, noisy home in the lower-class neighborhood.

Nine people lived in my house, including six kids brought in by different marriages. We constantly butted heads and had shouting matches.

I looked at the clock. Though he would only be in the house for a few minutes, I cringed at having him see the dirty carpet, the banged-up walls, and the hole my stepfather had kicked in the door. More than that, I prayed that no fights would break out. My disabled stepfather, his elderly mother, and my mother argued continually.

To my intense relief no fights erupted while he was there and we went to the dance without incident. Though I was happy to go with him, I wondered how long it would last once he found out how different our worlds were.

I always faced that problem. I made friends with people, they found out about the real me, and they left. I had invited a few girls from church to our home, but after they saw how I lived, the unspoken agreement was that all play dates would be at their houses. I was happy for a chance to escape to a world where each person had her own bedroom, allowance, new cars in the driveway, and stability.

I, on the other hand, shared a room with two sisters, and all nine of us crammed into a green Pontiac. When we unloaded from our car, as one friend remarked, we looked like a magic trick where you pulled out one handkerchief only to find that 10 more were attached.

As my friends got older they became more interested in shopping and eating out. I went along, though I never had any money. After all, we were the family that received food baskets at Thanksgiving. I tried to pretend that I was like my friends and go along with the glamour and chatter, but it all seemed remote from my life. Now at 15, I was painfully aware of how little I fit in.

**It seemed like there were two roads: one of ease and luxury where the normal people walked and one of pain.**

I often questioned God about this. It seemed like there were two roads: one of ease and luxury where the normal people walked and one of pain, like mine, where every day was a battle of survival. Whenever I attempted to cross to the other road I was soon forced back where I belonged. Even George stopped going out with me after a year.

Then one day at church my life changed. I was sitting in the balcony trying to join the whispering, giggling cluster of the other teens when suddenly the lights went out and a screen lowered. A missionary from India showed slides of the clinic he had set up to help outcast children. Cleft palates, deformed hands, and other disabilities barred these children from society. Though the deformities were correctable by surgery, most of the children were orphans or could not afford the medical costs. This clinic helped them get the operations.

I sat transfixed by the images of misery compared to the pictures of the transformed children who had received surgery, their faces glowing with health and contentment. My eyes filled with tears. Though I could never fully understand their poverty and despair, I did understand their loneliness and isolation. Suddenly I felt a fierce desire to help them.

My reaction surprised me. I had never thought about being a missionary. I wasn't even sure I fit that title. I only knew that the desire to make a difference was stirring in my heart. This revelation cast a faint glimmer of light on my dark path of pain. Maybe I didn't fit in because I wasn't supposed to. It was a strange shift in my thinking and I could hardly grasp it.

The lights came on and we sang a final hymn. The group of chattering teens I was with walked to McDonald's and I sat down, lost in the wonder of this new vision of myself. I had no money as usual, but for the first time it did not bother me. Instead of sitting wrapped in self-pity or trying to make small talk, I rejoiced at the glimpse I had into my life's purpose.

Maybe I didn't have money or popularity, but I had something more precious—the knowledge that God could use me. I didn't know how or when he would, but I knew my path had changed forever and I would never be the same.

*C. J. Sylraen*

## WHEN GOD
### breaks through

Perhaps you wonder why everyone seems to have it better than you. When you're tempted to have a pity party, consider these words from Jesus' Sermon on the Mount: "Blessed (happy, to be envied, and spiritually prosperous—with life-joy and satisfaction in God's favor and salvation, regardless of their outward conditions) are the poor in spirit (the humble, who rate themselves insignificant), for theirs is the kingdom of heaven!" (Matthew 5:3, AMP).

### my
## CHALLENGE

Make a list of the people, situations, or things you are thankful for. You don't have to create a long list or an I-*should*-be-thankful-for-these list. What aspects of your life cause you the most gratitude?

# SERVICE 21

## combining **FAITH** and action

The day promised good things. I woke up at a decent time instead of my usual late. Mom and I had a lucid discussion on the way to school. During band practice no one irritated our band director by goofing around during warm-ups.

As I sat in government class, halfway paying attention, something nudged me mentally. I started thinking about telling other people about who Jesus was and what he meant to me.

I attended church. I participated in Sunday school, afternoon discipleship group, and youth choir. In each of those settings I could easily talk about my spiritual life. But most of those people already knew Christ as their Savior.

The bell rang and I ambled off to chemistry. I liked this class better, so I paid more attention. Plus it was more difficult, and if I didn't concentrate I'd miss something important. In a spare moment, I surveyed who among my friends probably didn't know Jesus, but I just didn't see any way I could talk to them about religious stuff.

At lunch I sat with my best friends Billy, Anthony, Ron, and Derick. We cut up as usual. No serious conversations allowed in the lunchroom. Too many listening ears. I knew Anthony and Ron attended church, but I didn't know if Billy or Derick did. The typical question "If you died tonight, would God let you into heaven?" felt bloated with pressure and guilt, rather than grace and salvation. I knew hell was part of the equation; but it wasn't a normal topic my friends and I discussed.

Lunch, as always, seemed too short. My stomach felt queasy. I didn't know if that was because of the fries I'd stolen off Derick's plate or because of the guilt that was growing in me from not knowing my friends' spiritual status.

We headed our separate ways. Ron, Anthony, and I went to English while Billy and Derick went—I didn't even know where.

English class passed with no solution to my problem. I felt a burden to tell someone about Jesus, but I couldn't figure out whom to approach. I separated my choices into three groups: my friends who attended church, but might not know Jesus;

**I felt a burden to tell someone about Jesus, but I couldn't figure out whom to approach.**

my good friends who didn't attend church; and acquaintances about whose spiritual condition I didn't have a clue. As I headed toward the band hall, I discarded the acquaintances with a shiver, knowing I would never follow through with them.

Since it was marching season, I stayed after school for band practice. I put together my tenor saxophone and slogged through the heat that clings to Texas in the fall. I didn't think about religious matters; I was too busy trying to march in step and playing the song to the beat.

After band practice, Ron and I headed to the journalism room to finish the school newspaper and then deliver it to the printer. Here was my perfect opportunity, I thought. I always felt comfortable talking to Ron. I knew he went to church, but perhaps his relationship with Christ could use some encouragement. At least I could break the ice with him and see how I did at explaining spiritual life. I waited until we were in his truck on the road to the printer's office.

"Uh, Ron? What do you believe about God?"

He stared at me. "What?" he finally asked.

I started to sweat. My question was a good opener and not offensive, but already this was going badly.

"What do you believe about God?" I repeated.

He looked at me suspiciously. "Why do you want to know?"

*This is harder than I expected. What does he mean by that?* "Well, I was just wondering." I tried to shrug it off and searched for another topic. This wasn't going at all like I'd planned.

Ron looked pensive and then delivered the blow. "Dave, I don't really want to talk about religious stuff with you. I've seen how you act around girls. You're always cussing and saying raunchy stuff that's definitely not Christian. So I don't see what the point would be."

Stunned I almost retaliated with a few of those non-Christian words, but I didn't have a thing to say. I let the subject drop, wondering why God had put it on my heart all day long to share Jesus with someone.

Later at home that day, I realized God had a message for *me*, not Ron. God wanted me to know my witness had two parts—words and actions—and I wasn't practicing either.

It brought me to a point of prayer: *I want to do better in my attitude and language. Help me Lord.*

I wish I could say I immediately changed. But I continued to struggle in my walk. Rather than waiting until I achieved perfection, however, I used that struggle as a part of my witness. From time to time as I remember that conversation with Ron, I always think about the need to check both parts of my witness in my efforts to reach others for Christ.

*David W. Barnett*

## WHEN GOD
### breaks through

We may say, "Actions speak louder than words." James, the brother of Jesus, said it this way: "What good is it, my brothers, if a man claims to have faith but has no deeds? . . . Faith by itself, if it is not accompanied by action, is dead" (James 2:14–17, NIV). Pretty strong words, but others quickly notice when one of the two—faith or actions—is missing.

## my
## CHALLENGE

Got the guts to ask someone to evaluate whether or not your talk matches your walk? Talk to a friend and ask him or her to give examples of ways you practice what you preach.

# SHEEP, GOATS, AND A PAIR OF SHOES 22

## learning the **TRUTH** about God's kingdom

I wasn't surprised to be stuck carrying a heavy pair of athletic shoes around a crowded theme park on a hot July day. They weren't my shoes. I was wearing *my* shoes. These shoes belonged to the new guy.

I'm the kind of person the younger kids in my youth group lean on—they talk to me about what's on their minds, tell me their problems, and ask for advice (which I don't always have). Sometimes they ask me to go to our youth leader for them about a problem or with a request. Often I love this "mothering" role, listening and giving advice and being in charge, but sometimes I wonder if it really means I'm not much fun.

On this trip the new kid had come with someone. I don't even remember the boy's name—I just remember that he was working hard to fit in, and his big, clunky shoes didn't help. Somehow he borrowed some other shoes to wear, but that left those big, hot (and smelly) high-tops for someone to carry.

So he asked me. Granted, it wasn't a big sacrifice—the lines for my favorite rides were way too long. The issue wasn't the shoes; my role in the group bothered me. Why did I always get stuck carrying the shoes? When would it be OK for me to say, "Carry your own shoes! I want to do my own thing"? At what point could I stop taking care of everybody else and have fun?

Besides being responsible for my age, I was also thinking about things. I like figuring out why things work the way they do and why *I* work the way I do. So I walked around all day carrying those shoes and thinking.

I decided this wasn't a time to say, "No." I wanted this kid to have a good

time. I liked being able to take some worry off his shoulders and I already had done what I wanted to do at the park.

Then I thought of the story Jesus told about the final judgment. It convinces me that God really does bring some thoughts to our minds. In that story some people (the sheep) were welcomed into the kingdom, but others (the goats) were not. The king in the story said something like this to the sheep: "Come into my kingdom because you showed me kindness. You clothed me. You gave me water. You visited me when I was in prison."

"We don't remember doing those things," the sheep say. "When did we do those things for you?"

On this particularly hot afternoon, thinking about the king's answer to that question made a big difference in my day. "When you did it for the least of these my brothers," he said, "you did it for me."

In God's kingdom the small kindnesses *really* matter. If Jesus had asked me to carry his shoes for a few hours, would I have minded? No. It would have seemed like an important job, carrying Jesus' shoes around a theme park. I wouldn't have felt put upon; I would have felt chosen. If I adjusted my attitude just a bit, that's exactly what I was doing in the theme park. I was being kind to someone in Jesus' name, and this someone was just about the least in our group. He was new. He was struggling to fit in. He was out of his comfort zone.

> **In God's kingdom the small kindnesses *really* matter.**

After I processed this insight, I felt better. The shoes weren't any lighter, and they didn't smell any better. I'm sure we headed back to the bus eventually and I gave the kid back his shoes. Maybe he said thanks. Maybe not. But I was in service *with* God and *for* God and I understood in a new way what the kingdom of God is all about.

*Carol Smith*

# WHEN GOD
## breaks through

Sometimes we think that without an outgoing personality and a leadership role in our church group, at school, or on the team, we aren't contributing much. Unless we're organizing the food drive or leading a campaign to clean up the school parking lot, unless we're doing something *great,* we just aren't making a difference in our world.

The big things are not all that matter in God's kingdom; the small things also count—like the kind word you say to the girl who messes up her audition for the school play or the invitation you offer the new kid to sit with you and your friends at the basketball game. It's the dollar you give to the boy who comes up short in the lunch line. The small kindnesses make a huge difference, whether others realize it or not.

Even if no one else will ever know, you can count on Jesus to know exactly what you did. Because when you do a small kindness for someone else, you are, in fact, doing it for Jesus. Remember what the king said:

> *Then those "sheep" are going to say, "Master, what are you talking about? When did we ever see you hungry and feed you, thirsty and give you a drink? And when did we ever see you sick or in prison and come to you?" Then the King will say, "I'm telling the solemn truth: Whenever you did one of these things to someone overlooked or ignored, that was me—you did it to me"* (Matthew 25:37–40, MSG).

## my
## CHALLENGE

Wherever you are today—in the classroom, on the school bus, on the playing field, or at home—look for simple acts of kindness you can do for someone. Challenge yourself to do at least one kind thing for someone you don't know very well.

## learning to **ACCEPT** yourself

"All right, Bryant! That's enough. Next?"

Coach Johnson's whistle singled me out and confirmed what I hoped would not happen. My face burned with embarrassment as I left the badminton court. Only the ones who hadn't made it were called out while the rest of the girls continued playing until the best players were identified.

I fought tears as I yanked off my shorts and got dressed. I could not believe I had failed again. Since transferring from a small private school to this new public high school, I had been carefully instructed by my friends how to be college material. I was to try to get on the student body leadership team, do well in my classes, and get involved in sports. I was 16 and still had time to work my way to the top.

So for six months I tried in vain to get on some sort of team. I practiced relentlessly—running laps, shooting baskets, and doing whatever was necessary to be selected for a team. All to no avail. I failed at tennis, basketball, volleyball, and now badminton.

As I left the locker room I saw my friend Helen exultantly giving high fives to her other buddies who had made it. She caught my eye and looked sympathetic, but I turned away, hating her sympathy. It wasn't her fault I was such an oaf.

*Why God? Why couldn't I at least have made the badminton team?*

I was startled to hear an answer, a strange thought that popped into my head and didn't even relate to the question: *Birds don't gallop and horses don't sing.*

*That's weird. Where did I get that idea?* Then the meaning of the strange words came to me more clearly: *Sports are not your talent. Try something you do well.*

I stopped in the hall, startled at the revelation. *What am I good at?* Until then I had only seen sports as a viable option. All that evening I struggled with the answer. As I assessed my activities, I realized I was doing well in most of my classes, but struggled in geometry. So, academics didn't seem to be the answer. I didn't know my classmates well enough to win the next student leadership elections. What, if anything, was my talent?

The next day a tall, beautiful girl named Angelique hurried to me before classes started.

"Colleen, guess what?" she bubbled. "I'm **What, if anything,** hosting a talent show and I need people to be in **was my talent?** it. Can you do anything?"

In a flash it occurred to me: I can sing! I wondered why I hadn't thought of it before. I had been singing in church since I could walk.

Angelique's brown eyes watched me anxiously.

"Well, I guess I could sing," I admitted.

"Great!" Angelique exclaimed and signed me up.

The week before the talent show I was still struggling with what to sing. The only songs I knew were Christian songs. As I watched others practice the latest pop songs and magic tricks, I felt insecurity seeping into my soul. *You will never fit in here,* it said. *As soon as you open your mouth people will know you are a Christian loser as well as a sports failure.*

However, I knew I had to sing something from my heart—even if I failed. A friend showed me her accompaniment tapes and I found a song that seemed to fit me perfectly—"The Warrior Is a Child," by Twila Paris. The song is about someone who is trying to be strong, but is like a child inside and needs her heavenly Father to give her strength. It couldn't have been more fitting.

For the past six months I had struggled to be something I thought I should be, but failed miserably. Each time I ran to God, he picked me up and showed me that he made me the way I was for a reason. Though I wasn't sure where this path would lead, God seemed to be guiding me along the way.

On the night of the talent show, I felt nervous, but as I began to sing the truth of the song hit home and my voice swelled with emotion as the words rang out in the darkened theater.

I was stunned at the end of the show to find that I had won.

Soon I began to get requests to perform. Ironically I was asked to sing the national anthem at many of the sporting events in which I'd longed to participate. Though I would never be an athlete in those events, I was content because I had found my place and accepted the way God had made me.

The bird finally stopped trying to gallop and began to sing.

*Colleen J. Yang*

## WHEN GOD
### breaks through

Like Colleen, maybe you have wondered, *What's good about me?* or *What can I do well?* Even if you're not sure, David, the former shepherd turned conquering king, assures you that God always knows. "Nothing about me is hidden from you! I was secretly woven together deep in the earth below, but with your own eyes you saw my body being formed. Even before I was born, you had written in your book everything I would do" (Psalm 139:15–16, CEV). He knows when you triumph and when you fail. And he still loves you regardless.

## my
## CHALLENGE

List your strengths. Ask a friend or family member for feedback. You might be surprised at how long your list is. Consider ways you can use your strengths to encourage others. This week follow through on what you have decided.

# HARVESTING JOY 24

## trusting **GOD** in times of change

Every summer as I was growing up, our family spent a week at a hotel in Madison, Wisconsin. My parents attended a conference for my dad's campus ministry while my sister and I swam in the pool and watched reruns on TV.

On Sunday the conference held an informal church service in the hotel. For years during those services, I swung my legs over the folded chairs in the banquet room and thought about swimming that afternoon. But the summer after I graduated from high school, I was wondering how I would ever find my way when I started college in the fall.

Being between seasons of life can be lonely. My high school friends and I planned to stay in touch, but we knew we would eventually scatter and adapt to the foreign rhythms of adulthood—jobs, college, travel, marriage. Like thousands of others my age, I'd soon travel hundreds of miles away from home to live with people I didn't know, find classes in strange buildings, and try to figure out what I would do the rest of my life.

I wondered if the year ahead would offer me more peace than I had experienced in school so far. I'd carved out a small niche in high school, but rejection and insecurity punctured those years. The coming fall was my chance to be someone new—but I didn't know who that person was or how I would discover her. What if I never found a place where I belonged?

I was sinking deeper into my thoughts that Sunday when one of the speakers read a Bible verse I didn't recognize: "He who goes out weeping, bearing the seed for sowing, shall come home with shouts of joy, bringing his sheaves with him" (Psalm 126:6, ESV).

*Weeping* certainly was part of my life in high school as I struggled to meet teachers' requirements and tried to find my place among peers. Tears were also a big part of leaving high school, as I wondered what would come next. *Home* had new meaning for me now; soon I would be far from the people I loved. So the idea that it was all right to leave home weeping, with hopes to sow, was freeing. And I loved the image of returning home with joy, carrying the sheaves of hopes.

I kept that verse close to me all summer as my mom and I cruised back-to-school sales at the mall, and as I sorted through overly cheerful welcome letters from my new school.

**Weeping certainly was part of my life in high school.**

When my parents pulled away from my dorm in August, I was ready to gather whatever good things would come to me there.

I was devastated when my roommate and I did not connect. We got along in the sense that I ironed her shirt while she raced around getting ready for a date and she put up with my setting the alarm clock *hours* before my first class just because I like mornings. We both tried to be kind, but our schedules and personalities led beyond frustration to anger and sleeplessness and (on my part) many pathetic calls home. All my fears about not fitting in were coming true.

When a new friend, Kara, asked me to move in with her a few weeks later, I hesitated to believe that someone else might accept me when I felt so unacceptable. I knew that simply changing my living situation would not fix my apparently fatal flaws. Still our dorm leader encouraged me to accept Kara's offer, so I did.

I was not surprised that my roommate eagerly helped me move out my bedding and suitcases and crates of belongings, but I was amazed that Kara and a swarm of her friends showed up to help me move in. I had met several of Kara's friends before, but I had little more to say than thank you as they each trekked a load of my belongings across campus. Kara bought a potted plant to christen my side of the room as my new home. We fell into an easy routine, even with our different studies and hours, and I soon relaxed into the acceptance Kara gave. She also ushered me into a new group of friends who offered the laughter and security I'd hungered for.

When I returned home at Thanksgiving, I was full of stories about my college classes and relationships. The school year so far had not been what I had hoped that summer Sunday at the hotel. But Jesus had been present with me in more significant ways than I had imagined, even as I sowed in tears and waited for new life.

*Elisa Fryling Stanford*

# WHEN GOD
## breaks through

Maybe you are at an in-between time right now—waiting to begin high school, anticipating the start of a new school year and a clean slate, hoping to meet new people and make new friends. These ordinary events of our lives can be filled with all the emotion and hope and pain of greater events to come. These are the seeds we sow for the future. In many instances we will water those seeds with our tears of frustration and disappointment. But as Elisa learned, God can care for us while we're in that in-between time and can turn our sadness into a harvest of joy.

"May those who sow in tears reap with shouts of joy," the psalm writer wrote. "He who goes out weeping, bearing the seed for sowing, shall come home with shouts of joy, bringing his sheaves with him" (Psalm 126:6, ESV).

## my
## CHALLENGE

What are you waiting for right now? What do you hope will happen? Write this on a piece of paper, date it, and put it aside to look at in the future to see how God has brought a harvest of joy.

## mending a **BROKEN** heart

"Have you ever been in love?"

A week into classes my freshman year, I was tired of asking and answering questions about what town I grew up in and what my major was. I wanted to get to know my classmates on a more personal level. So I began to ask people three questions: What is your favorite crayon color? If you could eat only one food for the rest of your life what would it be? Have you ever been in love?

Asking these questions worked better than I expected.

Not only did I start to get to know a whole lot of girls in my dorm, but I also started getting to know a lot of cute guys. One especially caught my attention. His name was Tim, and he was tall, dark, and handsome. (OK, OK, it's a cliché, but he was!) Tim was musical, athletic, and creative. As he answered my three questions, I began to blush and giggle for no reason at all. It was nauseating, yet somehow wonderful.

I caught myself daydreaming about Tim. I wanted to know what his favorite movie was. I wondered what he wanted to do with his life. I imagined what it would be like to hold his hand. I hoped he would ask me out on a date soon!

Finally, as I was sitting with a group of girlfriends, he asked if I wanted to have dessert at McDonald's. That wasn't exactly the romantic rendezvous I had envisioned, but I eagerly accepted with a nod and a goofy smile. As Tim walked away, my friend chucked a goldfish cracker at my forehead. "Quit smiling like that," she insisted. "You look creepy!"

From that moment on my smile continued to grow. Before long Tim and I began to date each other exclusively. Many nights we stayed up, hot chocolate in hand, talking about anything and everything imaginable until the sun illuminated the sky. Tim serenaded me with lyrical love songs on the guitar. I drew him pictures of the two of us. We walked hand-in-hand on a starlit beach and rode horses up the side of a mountain. It was cheesy, yet romantic, and I knew I was in love.

Then one day it all ended abruptly with the four words every girl dreads: "We need to talk."

Tim guided me outside to a bench near my dorm. We sat down and he began the conversation I never wanted to have.

"I don't want to be in a relationship anymore," he said. "I want to do so many things and having a girlfriend prevents me from doing them."

I stared at Tim in confusion as my heart sank to the bottom of my stomach. I thought we were happy. I didn't understand. Surely we had an alternative to breaking up. "Maybe we could ..."

"No," Tim said, "it's over."

After a few moments of uncomfortable silence, we hugged goodbye. Tim got into his car and drove away. I watched the taillights fade into the distance. For a long time I sat alone on the bench, shivering in the dark, letting the tears stream down my face.

I cried myself to sleep that night, trying to figure out what I had done wrong or what I could have done

**One day it all ended abruptly with the four words every girl dreads: "We need to talk."**

differently. For the next few weeks, the breakup slowly consumed my life. Some days I felt like staying in my pajamas and eating an entire tub of ice cream. Other days I didn't want to eat at all. Some days I stayed in bed crying, hoping the ache in my stomach would disappear. Other days I wanted to get in my car and drive away fast, leaving the memories and pain behind. My grades started slipping. I stopped hanging out with my friends.

Eventually my roommate, Tara, told me with tears in her own eyes. "Al, it hurts me to see you in so much pain. You need to let go and move on. Stop holding on to the past and be confident that God has something in store for you far greater than you can imagine."

Tara reached for her Bible. "Pile your troubles on GOD's shoulders—he'll carry your load, he'll help you out (Psalm 55:22, MSG)," she read as she grabbed my hand. "You are better than this. Life will go on, but not until you wash your face and get out of bed. Let go! Trust God in all areas of your life—even with dating."

Maybe she was right. I had let this broken relationship overwhelm my every waking moment. I had stopped doing things that were important to me. I had let special friendships disappear.

"Tara," I moaned, "I miss Tim."

"It's gonna take time," she warned, "but don't waste the rest of your life sitting around missing him. Life is too short."

"I know." I leaned on my roommate's shoulders. "Thank you."

Tara nudged me out of bed. I stood up, ready to face the world again.

"Catch!" Tara exclaimed as she threw a washcloth at my face. "Remember—wash away your tears and let God do the rest."

I headed toward the bathroom and took a deep breath. I knew it wouldn't be easy. A song, a place, a time of day would trigger those memories of my time with Tim. But somehow I also knew God would get me through this. And that was enough for me.

*Allison Asimakoupoulos*

# WHEN GOD
## breaks through

The prophet Isaiah wrote, "You will keep in perfect peace all who trust in you, all whose thoughts are fixed on you!" (Isaiah 26:3, NLT). What a powerful reminder when disappointments threaten to overwhelm us—whether it's a failed relationship, a rejection letter from our "dream school," or a close friend's betrayal. We all will face disappointments, failures, and troubles; it's part of living in this world. God doesn't promise to remove our troubles. He doesn't promise an instant fix to all our problems. Instead God promises that when we quit wallowing in self-pity, when we take our eyes off our circumstances and focus on him and his Word, he will give us "perfect peace." When you let the truth of God's unchanging love and his mighty power fill you, you will have the confidence to stand up, wipe your tear-stained face clean, and trust him to guide you through.

## my
## CHALLENGE

Look up the following verses: Psalms 9:10; 18:29; 34:19; and John 14:1. Write down the one that means the most to you right now (whether good or bad). Carry it around with you or take time to memorize it. When you feel you are going to buckle under the stress, remember God is on your side. Always.

## watching a life of **AUTHENTIC** faith

When you tend to be a troublemaker, having the FBI as your neighbor is the last thing you want!

Our new neighbors seemed normal enough. They piled out of an old, overloaded vehicle—five kids, three of them boys, all about my age. The moving truck arrived and I watched as their stuff came out. Wait, motorbikes! No, even better—dirt bikes!

Later that afternoon I found an excuse to be in the front yard to meet them. The boys and I awkwardly shook hands and exchanged names. Then James, the oldest, introduced his dad—the FBI agent! My heart sank. *Forget about making friends with them*, I thought, trudging back into the house. *No dirt bike riding for me.*

When James and his family moved in, I was running with a tough crowd and had a bit of illegal activity going on, so I avoided my new neighbors whenever possible. With the FBI across the street, all I wanted to do was keep a low profile. But James ended up in some of my classes.

James was easy to like. He was polite and treated everyone with respect, including the kids who typically were the targets of criticism and cruel humor. Kids like me. At first I tried to steer clear of him, but James kept talking to me as if he thought we should become friends. When you're an angry kid from a dysfunctional family, you tend to be mean, especially to those who seem to have it all together. But James kept being a friend, even when I wasn't. I would be cruel; James would like me anyway. I would be selfish; he would still be there.

From the fish symbol and the bumper stickers on the family's car and their long, loud prayers before the meals I ate with them, I knew that James and his family were Christians. That was another reason I didn't want to become friends with James. I was exposed to the "God thing" as a kid but rejected everything religious. Although I had learned that someone created me for a reason, cared for me, and took care of my sin issue, it was all too confusing, and I just never wanted to think about it.

Despite these obstacles James and I did become friends. We hung out, played ball, studied, and talked about girls. At times we talked about God and about the reality of Jesus, but I avoided those conversations most of the time. I knew James prayed for me, but I didn't understand why. I only knew that he hadn't walked away when I'd tried to make him. In time we did ride those dirt bikes.

As I looked at James and his brothers, I saw that they made good choices. They were not swayed by the culture and

**When you're an angry kid from a dysfunctional family, you tend to be mean.**

temptations that so easily got to me. They were secure in who they were. I had none of that.

What slowly brought me from denying God to knowing him was three young men who chose to model Jesus in what they said and did. They didn't quote Bible verses at me. They didn't lecture me. They simply lived what they believed, even when their parents and church leaders weren't around. They never let anyone copy their homework. They never swore, gossiped, ran down others, or used sarcasm.

James often took heat when guys teased him about being the "preacher boy," and about being naive and innocent. James just laughed it off. He and his brothers were the real deal all the time.

I should know. I watched him for three and a half years—that's a long time to keep up a show. Finally I asked James why he was so different. He gave the answer you would expect. "Christ," he said.

"Yeah, sure. I'm watching you," I replied.

I did watch—and it made all the difference in my life.

*Mike Brantley*

## WHEN GOD
### breaks through

What mattered most to Mike was the consistent and honest life that James and his brothers lived. That attracted Mike to Christ. Those same qualities will make a difference to the people who are watching you and evaluating the claims of the one you follow. As Paul advised Titus, "In the same way, encourage the young men to live wisely in all they do. And you yourself must be an example to them by doing good deeds of every kind. Let everything you do reflect the integrity and seriousness of your teaching" (Titus 2:6–7, NLT). When our words about God and our faith match our lives, others will listen to us talk about what we believe.

### my
## CHALLENGE

Think about the people in your life. Who is watching as you live out your faith? Remember the decisions you made, the words you spoke, and your actions over the past 24 hours. How did those decisions, words, and actions reflect your faith to others? What could you change to be a more effective, living example of Christ?

## endings mean **BEGINNINGS** too

My mother was dying. The doctors sent her home because they had no cure for her cancer. We had been sitting quietly in her bedroom for a long time.

"Your opinion matters a lot to me," she said. "You are wise and I trust you." Then she looked at me and asked, "Do you think I should stay or go?"

Two things went through my mind: One, that my life had been forever changed. Two, that no teenager should have to tell a parent it is OK to die.

Mom was waiting for words of wisdom that I knew I didn't possess. Instead of answering right away, I asked what she thought she should do.

"It would be easier to go because I am tired of fighting, but I think your dad wants me to keep fighting," she said.

My eyes filled with tears as I told her we all wanted her to be happy and it would be OK to stop fighting if she was ready to go be with Jesus.

She looked straight at me and said, "So you think I should go?"

I told her that we would all fight this with her if that was what she wanted. I told her that the daughter in me wanted her to fight and stay and be my mom, but the hope we have in Christ was allowing me to let her go be with Jesus if she was ready.

"I just wish I knew if I should stay or go," she said with a sigh.

I am struck by how fine the line is between the temporal and the eternal. Mom had no control over the cancer destroying her body, yet she fought and held on. Sometimes she would be totally coherent and talk easily. Moments later she hallucinated. I watched as chunks of her life moved through her memory and she tried to make sense of them. It's strange to watch the person who was there when you were born slowly leave the world. It's so painful and yet so intimate.

God kept giving her glimpses of heaven that calmed her. She told us how incredible all the flowers are. It's funny: I think of heaven as a realm so far away, yet it was so close to her. Her smile as she caught fleeting glimpses of heaven was soon the only emotion she showed.

Two days later my mom informed my brother and me, "I see him!" My brother asked who she saw, and she replied, "Jesus, I see Jesus. He is the kindest man I have ever seen. It's all true. All we believe is all true."

Through my tears I asked if Jesus was calling her, but she said no.

I told her that if he was calling, it was OK to go with him. In that moment I realized that I had released my mom to Jesus. I really did trust that heaven was the best place for her. I had never felt as confident about following Jesus as I did right then. I vowed to renew my efforts to share the gospel with others. There really is a beautiful eternity just beyond this life. I cannot imagine watching a loved one die with no hope of eternity and no glimpse of what God has waiting.

**It's strange to watch the person who was there when you were born slowly leave the world.**

Mom's voice broke into my thoughts. "Are you ready for me?" she asked Jesus. A moment later she told him, "I'm not ready yet." She was still fighting, and Jesus was giving her more time.

Eight days later, when the end finally came for my mom, it wasn't so much an end but a beginning. For her it was the beginning of a new and perfect life with Jesus. It was the beginning of a different life for those of us who love and miss her.

Growing up I could never imagine life without my mom. I still miss her terribly and some days I wish God had healed her and left her here for me. I divide my life between the times before and after Mom's death. In the years since she went home to heaven, my passion to know and be known by God has increased. Now I can never imagine life without Jesus.

As Mom said, "It's all true. All we believe is all true."

*Nina Edwards*

# WHEN GOD
## breaks through

Have you ever had a moment when you know what is happening right then will affect the rest of your life? You tell yourself that from now on your life will be split in two parts: what happened before this moment and what happens from this point on. That's what Nina experienced at her mother's death. Instead of being shattered, her faith was strengthened through the tragedy, thanks to the witness of her mom who was torn between wanting to stay on earth and wanting to be with Jesus. The apostle Paul knew that struggle. "I am hard-pressed between the two, having a desire to depart and be with Christ, which is far better. Nevertheless to remain in the flesh is more needful for you" (Philippians 1:23–24, NKJV). Staying was needful for Nina's faith.

Sometimes we're torn between wanting an easier experience and continuing through the hard realities of living the Christian life. To echo Paul's words, it is "more needful" to remain where we are. Ever feel like that? Someday, someone's faith may be strengthened by yours.

## my
## CHALLENGE

Think of an experience you would label "Before _____"
and "After _____." How did that experience change your life? What would you want others to know about God based on that?

# IN SEARCH OF WATER 28

## thirsting to **KNOW** Jesus

I was so out of breath I could barely stand. Doubling over on the grass, I felt my body start to shake. My heart was beating like crazy, and I struggled to speak.

"Time out!" I finally yelled. "I . . . need . . . some . . . water!"

"Who has water?" Peter yelled, looking around. His voice dropped. "Ann, I think we forgot to bring water."

"Are you kidding?" I asked. I was convinced that if I didn't get water soon, I would become seriously dehydrated.

After all it was the middle of July. I'd just finished my freshman year in college and was in Oxford, England, with 40 other students from my school. We were traveling around the United Kingdom for seven weeks, taking classes, sightseeing, and learning about English culture. I was having the time of my life and feeling very independent and mature.

We had gone to church that morning at St. Aldate's Cathedral, an ancient church building with a lively congregation. After the service Jon and Erin suggested we find a park and play Ultimate Frisbee. Over half of the group was up for it, so we trekked to a huge park on the edge of town. I'd never played Ultimate Frisbee before, but I was fairly athletic and I figured I could pick the game up quickly. We broke into two groups and huddled in separate circles to lay out our plans of attack.

I got totally into the game, diving after the disc and body checking the opposing team members whenever they got in my way. I was also sweating like crazy in the midday sun and I was getting sunburned.

"Peter, how could all 25 of us forget to bring water?"

"I don't know, but we did. I'm sure we can just head around the corner and buy some."

I groaned. Everything was expensive in England.

But when Peter and I panted to the street we found the shops were closed. We would have to walk at least a half hour back to our campus, and I wasn't sure if I could make it without a drink. Besides we couldn't start walking back into town without telling our friends who were still in the park.

"Peter, I really feel dizzy. I know there's nothing open, but I need to get some water—soon," I said. I prayed silently, asking God to provide some water as we headed back to the park.

Near the park entrance we noticed a church, and Peter said, "Ann, let's check out the church. They're sure to be open on a Sunday, right? Maybe we can find a drinking fountain or a restroom with a sink."

"If there's water in the building, I'm there."

The church was open, but completely empty—cool and silent. I leaned against the gray stones and felt my flushed cheeks. I had never been so thirsty in my life. We looked for five minutes for a "loo," as the English call it, but found no restroom.

**"I know there's nothing open, but I need to get some water—soon."**

"Peter, we're wasting time. Let's just get the rest of the group and head back. The sooner we leave, the sooner we can get to water."

"OK. Let's go."

We left through the back door of the church and started to walk toward the front. Then, on the side of the church, I spotted a water faucet. "Peter! Look!" I pointed to the faucet. "Do you think it works?"

The metal was rusty. Peter grabbed the nozzle and turned it to the left—hard. Brown water trickled out, but I gasped and plopped down near the faucet, relieved. When the water became cleaner, I stuck my head under the faucet, slurping water to my heart's content. Then I pulled back, and Peter got a drink too.

After another long gulp, I turned to Peter. "I've never tasted water this good in my life."

"I think that's because you're so thirsty. This water is actually pretty questionable, but I'm past caring."

I waited by the faucet while Peter went to our friends. I leaned back against the wall of the church, enjoying the shade. The church was the only place near the park with water available—free water.

Just like the springs of eternal life that Jesus provides.

And we just can't live without water.

*Ann Swindell*

## WHEN GOD
### breaks through

Remember what Jesus said to the Samaritan woman he had met at the well? "Everyone who drinks this water will be thirsty again, but whoever drinks the water I give him will never thirst. Indeed, the water I give him will become in him a spring of water welling up to eternal life" (John 4:13-14, NIV). Even though we can easily quench our thirst any time, an hour or so later, we will be thirsty again. The water on this earth can never last for long. But the "water" Jesus was talking about—the gift of his Holy Spirit and eternal life—lasts forever. That's the kind of water, like the water at the church, that is free for the taking because Jesus offers it to *anyone* who is thirsty. Only Jesus can satisfy our real thirst.

### my
## CHALLENGE

Think of three ways you are thirsting to know Jesus right now. Write them down and then ask him to satisfy your thirst for him today.

# finding a **MIRACLE** in a disaster

I was excited but scared when my youth group took a mission trip to New Orleans to help clean up the destruction from Hurricane Katrina. Would I be able to do the hard work? Could I conquer my fears and share the gospel if I received the opportunity? The butterflies fluttered in my stomach throughout the 16-hour drive from Indiana to New Orleans and into our first morning there.

That Monday morning I decided to join the group that would prepare an area school for the new school year. Another group would clean a house for a woman named Pam and her daughters. That whole day at the school, I regretted my decision. What was I afraid of? Cleaning the school was hard work and I was helping people, but I kept feeling God tugging at my heart. I promised myself that the next day I would work at the house.

Tuesday morning was hot and muggy; my long pants stuck to my legs as we drove to Pam's house. I had a bad feeling but tried to be optimistic. The thought of rescuers entering some of the homes we passed and finding bodies inside made me shudder. I tried not to think about it and concentrated on getting my boots on as we approached Pam's house.

Someone had hung an American flag on the front porch. At the edge of the road stood an enormous pile of rubbish. I scanned the heap and noticed a teddy bear and clothes with the tags still on them. I had to look away; I didn't want the rest of my group to see me cry. We gathered on the porch and prayed before we started working.

Clearing out the debris in that house was the hardest work I had ever done. The morning sped by. Our whole group was drenched in sweat, and just when the heat and exhaustion were starting to get to me and my enthusiasm had begun to slowly trickle away, someone yelled, "Pam is here!"

Pam slowly stepped around the pile of debris in her front lawn and walked to the front porch where we waited to see her. We greeted her with smiles and she smiled back. Our leader led her through the house so she could see how everything was coming along. Then Pam came back out and talked to us.

"Yesterday when I drove past the house with my daughters," she said, "I couldn't help but cry. I saw the flag on my porch and it just hit me—you look at this whole block of homes and see nothing but destruction, then you see my house and the flag. It just filled me with assurance. I want my house to be the first on this block cleaned out so people can see it as a beacon of hope. It can encourage them to rebuild and move on with their lives like I am doing. It's the start of a new beginning. I'll keep praying for you guys. Thank you so much."

Her eyes filled with tears, and I would have cried too if her words hadn't made me so happy. We had given her hope just by putting up a flag! After Pam left, our whole group was determined to get this house done for Pam and for God's glory.

**I want my house to be the first on this block cleaned out so people can see it as a beacon of hope.**

The rest of that week I went to the house each day and worked the hardest I could. Every time I felt like giving up, I thought about Pam and her daughters. They needed a home and they needed our help. By the end of the week, we had cleared out the whole house and put up a sign in front that said House of Hope. As we drove away I couldn't help but smile.

Who would ever think that God could use something as terrible and horrifying as Katrina to give hope to so many people?

*Kelsey Berry*

# WHEN GOD
## breaks through

What do you hope for? A better grade in history, an acceptance letter from the college of your dreams, a chance to make the team? We usually use the word *hope* to indicate something we want to occur, but aren't really sure if it will happen. But the hope Kelsey and her friends brought to Pam and others in the aftermath of the Katrina disaster was much more than a wish. It was a confident hope, a certain hope, based on the promise that God was at work in the middle of that disaster to help the people rebuild their lives. We can be confident and filled with hope that God will do exactly what he says. That's a hope that will not disappoint us.

> *Praise be to the God and Father of our Lord Jesus Christ! In his great mercy he has given us new birth into a living hope through the resurrection of Jesus Christ from the dead (1 Peter 1:3, NIV).*

## my
## CHALLENGE

Look up these verses about hope from the Old Testament: Psalm 33:18; Isaiah 40:31; Jeremiah 29:11; and Lamentations 3:25. Memorize one.

# A REASON TO PLAY 30

## finding **JOY** in discipline

Piano lessons were nonnegotiable in our household growing up. My sisters and I had to take lessons as a matter of *discipline*.

"You need the discipline to bring the joy," my father, the pastor, intoned.

I loved music, but I sure didn't find any joy in taking piano lessons!

"How long do I have to take these lessons?" I often asked.

"Until you can play every song in the hymnbook," he responded.

At the time I was thankful I didn't have to learn all of Beethoven, Bach, or Mozart!

I actually liked the hymns we sang in church. I had read the hymnbook from cover to cover many times; these songs told their own stories about fiery trials, battles, and being true to the end. I found them filled with adventure, faith, and wonder. Still, I had no interest in my piano lessons.

My father asked me to play for a small church that didn't have a regular piano player. This new responsibility forced me to practice. Now I had an audience, and sometimes a choir to accompany. I didn't want to embarrass myself or discourage anyone from singing. And then, I got a new teacher.

Mrs. Stewart occasionally filled in as the church organist. One day she took me to church for my lesson and introduced me to the fundamentals of playing the organ. She invited me to play a duet with her—she played the organ and I played the piano. *This* was fun.

Mrs. Stewart invited me to play with her the following Sunday morning. After the service she hugged me and said, "You did *very* well!" With that affirmation I began to embrace the hated Hanon piano drills and practiced more often for my lessons.

Additional encouragement came through a gift from my father: When I sat down to practice one day, there on the piano was a large songbook with all the songs of one of my favorite Christian artists. It was the *perfect* gift. Mrs. Stewart also encouraged me to play for our youth choir, and I introduced some of these new songs to the choir, which they loved.

Opportunities grew and so did my enthusiasm. During my freshman year at college, I played for the youth choir at the church I attended. Later I added another youth choir in a neighboring town. These combined youth choirs opened a concert for a well-known Christian artist touring in our area.

**You need the discipline to bring the joy.**

Sometimes, in the hush that trailed the end of a song, I could almost hear my father saying, "You need the discipline to bring the joy."

I occasionally visited an elderly woman, Mrs. Irene, who had played the piano for many years. "Play something for me," she always said. "Anything out of the hymnbook is fine."

I began to play and sing, and she hummed along. Soon she joined in singing, and I gave way to her rich alto voice, carrying the song as if we were on a happy road trip in the countryside.

Joy.

Occasionally other women in the community invited me to play for their special events—a ladies' tea or a birthday celebration. Each time they would ask, "Play us a hymn," and eventually everyone was singing.

More joy.

What was missing in my initial piano lessons was purpose. Because of my father's insistence on the discipline of learning to play, God could give me joy as I played for others.

I never became a great piano player; my skills remain intermediate at best. But I still pull out the hymnbook and sit down to play.

And it brings me joy.

*Karen Young*

# WHEN GOD
## breaks through

According to the *American Heritage Dictionary*, *discipline* is "training expected to produce a specific character or pattern of behavior, esp. training that produces moral or mental improvement." That definition alone is enough to cause an eye roll or two, especially when thoughts of a parent's "It's good for you" come to mind. But God would define *discipline* as a labor of love—his love for you. Just as Karen was urged to submit to her father's suggestion to continue practicing, we're urged to submit to God's discipline.

> *Don't shrug off God's discipline, but don't be crushed by it either. It's the child he loves that he disciplines; the child he embraces, he also corrects. God is educating you; that's why you must never drop out. He's treating you as dear children.... At the time, discipline isn't much fun. It always feels like it's going against the grain. Later, of course, it pays off handsomely, for it's the well-trained who find themselves mature in their relationship with God" (Hebrews 12:5–11, MSG).*

Discipline may come in the form of a quiet urge to pray or to change a habit. Discipline separates a disciple from an all-talk-and-no-action wannabe. Which are you?

## my
## CHALLENGE

In what ways do you sense God disciplining you? Perhaps he's calling you to spend time with him each day. Or perhaps he wants you to break a habit instead of starting one. Are you willing?

# discovering a **FATHER** who knows all secrets

Here it is!

Months earlier I'd sent away to get my birth certificate so I could enroll in a new school. Because my parents divorced when I was a baby, I don't have much information about my dad. But this was an opportunity to know his name and some official information about him.

I ripped the envelope and jerked the thick, ivory paper out of it. A gold-embossed state seal topped the paper. In messy, but legible handwriting, I saw my full name with birth date and time. The next line of boxes contained *Fulton County, Fulton County Hospital,* and *Atlanta*. I skimmed my mother's name and age to read the next line: *Father: Husband is not the father.*

*What? How could this be?* I felt dizzy from the questions that were spinning in my mind.

My foster mom, Mrs. Smith, was making dinner. She was only in her late twenties and had been mistaken by my principal and teachers as my sister. Even though she was just slightly more than a decade older than me, she was mature and had proved to be a good substitute mom. As she poured the chicken casserole into the baking dish, she was oblivious to my crisis.

I tossed the sheet in front of her, and she looked up with alarm.

"Do you think this will keep me from getting into school?" I'd been looking forward to attending a Christian school, so I tried to keep a poker face to hide my disappointment. As she read I dashed to my room so I wouldn't lose control in front of her.

As I sat cross-legged on the bed, tears streamed down my face. The year before Mom had sent me to live with my sister, her husband, and infant daughter in another state. I hung out with friends who cut school. If we got hungry we stole what we needed to fill our stomachs.

When my sister couldn't take care of me, my youth group leaders, the Smiths, had offered me a place to stay and the hope of a private school. Just when my life seemed to be taking a positive turn, it had crashed again—when I asked my mom for a birth certificate, she never mailed it to me. She said she forgot. Maybe it was because my mom had something to hide.

I looked at the pictures of my brother and sister in the top drawer of my nightstand. I stood in front of the mirror and compared the photos to myself. Megan and Rob had dark hair and a similar nose and mouth. My hair was auburn, and my face and arms were freckled.

**If the State of Georgia doesn't know who my dad is, who does?**

*Maybe we* don't *have the same dad. If the State of Georgia doesn't know who my dad is, who does?*

I decided to call my sister. "Hey Sis, I got my birth certificate today."

"Great! So when do you start at the new school?"

"Have you ever seen my birth certificate?"

"No. Why?"

"Do you know who my dad is?"

"Not exactly. It was some guy mom hung out with. I don't know his name or anything. You mean—you never knew we had different dads?"

The conversation left me with more questions. I couldn't call my mom; I knew she wouldn't tell me anything. So I called my Aunt Alice, my mom's sister and confidant. My aunt said Mom had dated several men about that time, and hinted that my mom wasn't sure who my father was. I hung up, devastated.

*Who is he?* I didn't have a clue. If my mom didn't know, then my father probably didn't even know I existed. The whole mess was infuriating.

"Does God know?" I cried out.

"Yes."

I looked around to see if someone had come into my room. No one. *Did I really hear something?*

When I was younger Mom sent us to church. I had some good Sunday school teachers who told Bible stories about God talking to people. One teacher told my class about a boy named Samuel, who kept hearing someone call his name (see 1 Samuel 3). Eli the priest told him that God must be calling him. He instructed Samuel to answer God and listen to his words. Remembering that I prayed, *God, I just want to know who my dad is.* Then I waited for God to answer.

Though I still didn't know who my earthly father was I started searching the Bible to know my heavenly Father better. I started reading the Bible every day. Recently I read Daniel 2:22, "He reveals deep and hidden things; he knows what is in the darkness, and the light dwells with him" (ESV). This verse gives me hope because God knows who my dad is and will let me in on the secret if I need to know.

In the meantime, thanks to my heavenly Father, I soon learned that I was accepted into the Christian school and would receive a tuition waiver.

But when I get to heaven someday, I am going to ask to see the top secret file on my dad. I want to meet him.

*Sally Smith*

## WHEN GOD
### breaks through

Sally's experience shows that God doesn't always answer "Yes." Sometimes he says, "No," or "Wait." The apostle Paul, who wrote much of the New Testament, experienced God's "no." But he wasn't left hanging. "Three times I pleaded with the Lord about this, that it should leave me. But he said to me, 'My grace is sufficient for you, for my power is made perfect in weakness.' Therefore I will boast all the more gladly of my weaknesses, so that the power of Christ may rest upon me" (2 Corinthians 12:8–9, ESV).

Although Sally didn't learn the identity of her father, she learned that her heavenly Father wanted to take care of her. Through her experience she trusted God, his wisdom, and his timing.

### my
## CHALLENGE

What are you waiting for right now? Make a list of your concerns and requests, and date them. Next to that list add another column and label it "God's Answers." Review your list frequently (you might want to place it in your Bible) and record God's answers when you receive them. Ask God to encourage you and help you as you wait.

## seeing life from **GOD'S** perspective

Life had become one test after another. Normally a morning person, now I couldn't get out of bed. When Mom got me up for school, I just sat on the couch and cried. I couldn't focus on my schoolwork and didn't want to face my friends even though they supported me during these difficult times my family was facing.

My faith was being tested too. People at church said things like "Jesus is always walking with you" and "God will take care of you," but I wanted to scream at them "No, he's *not!*" "It's not fair!" and "If he is, then how come my life is like this?" I had grown up with the attitude that if I believed in God, life would always be easy and bad things just wouldn't happen to my family and me.

But I learned life's not like that.

My sophomore year had started perfectly—until an early morning phone call in the middle of September changed everything.

My dad called to tell my mother that he was being laid off. Mom started freaking out, but I figured she was overreacting. Dad would get another job.

"I need to hurry or I'll miss the bus. I'm sorry about Dad, but I'm sure he'll get another job," I said. And I was off.

By the time I got home, the cutbacks had begun. At a family meeting Mom and Dad explained how life would be different until my dad had another secure job. We would have no cable TV, no Internet, and no cell phones. The heat would be turned down, so we'd need to use extra blankets at night and dress more warmly around the house during the day.

I couldn't believe how unreasonable my parents were being. Didn't they know I had a quality of life to maintain? Could they even imagine how people would look at me when I told them I couldn't IM or that I didn't have a cell phone? It was unthinkable. How much difference could that bill for Internet service really make? How dare my parents alienate me from my friends?

What made life even more frustrating was that at age 15, I couldn't get a job. I depended on my parents for income, and now *they* didn't have much.

By the end of November, right around Thanksgiving, things were really tight. Our church stepped in to help, giving us groceries. While I was grateful for what they were doing for us, it was also humbling, embarrassing, and frustrating. Charity was for the poor—not for my family! And because it was Thanksgiving, people thought we needed lots of stuffing.

## Charity was for the poor —not for my family!

I don't like stuffing.

I was forced to look at how tough our situation actually was and realized that my life could change even more. My parents were talking about moving in with Grandma if things didn't improve, which would mean selling our house and possibly going to a different high school the next year.

Around that time my dad found a low-paying factory job, but he hated it and quit after a week to keep looking for other options. Every Sunday our family bawled through the service because we were so overwhelmed with everything—the uncertainty of our situation and other people's generosity.

I tried to stay positive for my family. My brother Ben took it hardest. Only 11 years old and with learning disabilities, he didn't understand what was happening. Easily frustrated, he would flip to his favorite TV channel only to remember that the cable was gone. Then he'd start crying hysterically. He had a hard time at school, complaining to his teacher about what was happening and staying in a downward spiral, sometimes for days.

Christmas was coming and that's when it really hit home that my dad's job was gone. Our stockings hung empty and it was hard to focus on Jesus' birth instead of presents. Christmas was nowhere near our usual celebration with food, a real tree, and lots of *stuff*.

Dad found another job just before Christmas. The pay wasn't great, but he had opportunity to advance. Our earlier lifestyle was still beyond us, but things started to look up after the holidays. My family felt more positive and cried less often. That's when I fell apart. The emotional roller coaster of embarrassment, fear, and gratitude had worn me out.

In February my mom took me to a therapist, and I was diagnosed with depression. I started a series of counseling sessions that helped me deal with reality. I learned to face the truth of what my family was going through and accept help from others. And I learned that life is both good and bad. My therapist was so helpful I think she may have been an angel in human form!

In March my dad was promoted to supervisor, and our finances started looking up. We still had to be careful with our money and we still received help from others, but we were beginning to get back to making it on our own.

Meanwhile I learned a few lessons—it's OK to take humbling jobs and ask others for help. The church family is there so we can help each other through rough times. And my view of Jesus has changed too.

I now realize what I couldn't see then—he's always there for us, in the good times and in the bad.

*Brooke A. as told to Heather Pleier*

# WHEN GOD
## breaks through

When hard times hit, a pat answer from someone who doesn't know how you feel might make you mad instead of grateful. "Keep hope alive!" "Don't give up!" *Yeah right,* you might think.

David, one of the kings of Israel and an ancestor of Jesus, was no stranger to discouragement. Like Brooke, he knew life is "both good and bad." He spent years being chased by a man who wanted him dead. Yet even through those experiences, he wrote, "Why are you downcast, O my soul? Why so disturbed within me? Put your hope in God, for I will yet praise him, my Savior and my God" (Psalm 42:11, NIV). He could write that and mean it because he believed it.

When difficulties leave you discouraged, you have two options: doubt and despair, or trust that God can somehow make even the hardest times worthwhile.

## my
## CHALLENGE

Discouraged? Read Psalm 42. Think about what it says. Even if you can't believe that God could possibly redeem your situation, are you willing to hang on to him? Take a few moments to be real with God.

## sharing the **GIFT** of God's love

When I was 15, I loved my hometown of Southaven, Mississippi. But then my dad landed a job in Loredo, Texas. I didn't want to leave my hometown. It was all I knew, and I didn't want to leave. But we moved from the land of Elvis to the land south of El Paso.

My mom, my dad, and I lived in an apartment. I had a swimming pool, no yard to mow, and was within walking distance of my school. Also that year, Mom and Dad had their twenty-fifth wedding anniversary, I made about a dozen friends and I got a tan for the first time in my life. I was to discover the delectable taste of fajitas—marinated for hours and slow-cooked over mesquite wood. Life was *good*.

Life was different for my mother. She was unhappy as a stranger in a strange place. I listened to her talk as she struggled to understand this nonegalitarian culture and lamented about how much she missed the green grass of Graceland. (That is, North Mississippi.)

Mom was more homesick than Dad and I. But soon she found someone she could relate to who lived in the arid climate: Wylie Coyote. Yes, she loved the crafty cartoon canid that messed up every plan he conceived.

It was ridiculous, but Mom and I religiously watched this absurd cartoon every Saturday morning. Together we howled at his unquenchable desire for the Roadrunner. The sound no faithful follower can ever forget was the slow whistle of Wylie falling from some great height, so stupefied by the turn of events that he wouldn't utter a single sound before he hit the ground with a resounding thud. *POW!*

But we knew Wylie would be all right. We'd see him again next week. So we laughed and laughed until tears slid down our faces.

For that first Christmas in Texas, I decided to get Mom something memorable: I bought her a stuffed Wylie Coyote. I wrapped it and placed it under the tree nervously, not sure if she would think it was too childish. I argued with myself about getting such a silly gift. More than once I thought I should have gotten her perfume.

On Christmas morning, as we stood around in our robes, I gingerly handed my present to her. "Here, uh, Mom. I hope you like it."

I held my breath as she opened the box, carefully laying aside the wrapping paper.

Then my mother, a former professional portrait artist and businesswoman, squealed like a little girl.

**I had expected a tolerant laugh, but this was *way* above and beyond.**

"You like it?" I asked, dumbfounded.

"Oh, honey! It's wonderful!" She kissed me on the cheek, and cuddled the coyote. She laughed. "Look at those eyes! Those crazy ears! Oh thank you, honey!"

I was amazed. I had expected a tolerant laugh, but this was *way* above and beyond. If I'd given her a Tiffany diamond, I could not have gotten a better reaction from her.

Something weird was going on—a 49-year-old woman shouldn't be so excited over a stuffed animal.

But Jesus knew what he was doing.

We didn't know it at the time, but Norma Joyce Carmon had cancer. In less than three months, mere weeks after her fiftieth birthday, she would have a full mastectomy. That sounds bad, doesn't it? It was.

As we visited my mother in the hospital after her surgery, she had one firm request: "Please bring me my Wylie!"

We obeyed.

There she sat, this wild Irishwoman, propped up by pillows, brushing her coyote's ears and laughing. I've thought about that a lot. I believe as she sat laughing, God was filling her heart so she could run the terrible race before her. The coyote would sit beside her in that antiseptic hospital room, accepting Mom as she was, not as she wanted to be. He would be fuzzy just for her. He would be silly just for her. He would let her hold him as closely as she needed to when she wept alone at night.

I've often thought about that Christmas morning—the joy of that strange present. I think a little bit of Jesus was in that coyote because it is impossible for a 16-year-old boy to get such a perfect gift in his own wisdom. No, it was Jesus. It was too timely, too perfect. I didn't know him at the time, but he knew Mom. Jesus used me. And a coyote for Christmas.

*Justice Carmon*

## WHEN GOD
### breaks through

Many of us have an image of God as a stern, no-nonsense judge. Consequently we might not think God would use something we would call "silly" to make someone's day. Ever feel that way? But as James, Jesus' brother, assures us, "Every good and perfect gift is from above, coming down from the Father of the heavenly lights, who does not change like shifting shadows" (James 1:17, NIV).

### my
## CHALLENGE

Justice's gift made a huge difference in his mom's life. What have you given to someone (a gift, a word of encouragement, a smile) that caused a similar reaction? If you had the opportunity to brighten someone's day, what would you do? Why not ask God for the opportunity to do so.

# finding your **IDENTITY** through the love of God

"You look like a natural hiker," my math teacher's wife told me as we started our descent into the Bolivian jungle.

I was proud that she called me a hiker. I had a bright blue external frame backpack strapped securely to my shoulders so I looked like a hiker. And I relished being thought of as this kind of outdoors woman.

Hiking wasn't anything new to me. I was 15 and lived in Bolivia where my dad directed a youth camp outside the city of Cochabamba. My family often camped and hiked. My sisters and I always explored the outdoors wherever we were: building forts, making dams, and using found objects to create items.

Now for my high school's annual fall camping trip, we were hiking the Inca Trail from the capital city of La Paz to Los Yungas, the lowland river basin. I was ready to show everyone I was indeed the natural hiker I looked like.

Besides looking forward to showing off my hiking prowess, I bought crazy red and white striped cotton pants for this adventure. I looked like a giant candy cane with the red and white stripes running down the legs. They weren't the best pants for blending into the natural environment, but who wanted to blend in? I was known for wearing funky pants and had a reputation to maintain, even on a hiking trip.

We started our hike at 15,000 feet in the snowcapped Andes Mountains and ended it three days later among banana trees at 4,000 feet.

The Inca Indians had built extensive road systems throughout Bolivia and

Peru before the Spaniards conquered them. As the sun rose on the first day, we descended one of those cobblestone roads. We marveled that the rock steps and sidewalks were still in place 500 years later.

While hiking, our group quickly divided. Most of the boys raced ahead with our teacher, while I stayed behind with my girlfriends. By the time my "slower" group arrived at the campsite, the boys had set up most of the tents and were playing soccer.

My knees hurt after stepping down, down, down all day and I just wanted to rest. But something else also bothered me. When I started that day, I told myself I wanted to hike with my friends, no matter how fast or slow they went. I wasn't going to try to keep up with the first group. By the end of the day, I realized if I wanted to be known as a natural hiker, I needed to keep up with the first group—with all my fast and fit classmates.

The next day I tried to keep up with the "fast" group, but I couldn't. With each step I got farther behind and my discouragement grew.

*I'm a camp director's daughter*, I mused. *I should be near the front.*

As we descended into the jungles and banana trees, the temperature grew hotter. I was glad I had worn lightweight pants. A few hours later, we reached a steep, uphill section. This felt great for my knees, yet breathing was now difficult.

We hiked in one long line, trying to stay together. I was near the front and couldn't catch my breath, but didn't want to stop. I wanted to prove I could stay among those leading. The hotter my face got, the harder I pushed. The more I thought about how I should be able to do this, the more I wanted to cry.

Finally, with tears choking my throat and my face red and burning, I grabbed my friend's arm. "I can't breathe!" I gasped.

"Stop! Everyone, stop! Johannah can't breathe!" someone said.

Immediately my friends surrounded me, fanning me, offering me water, and telling me to take deep breaths.

"You must be hyperventilating," someone suggested. "Drink lots of water. We don't want you to dehydrate and faint."

4

I was so embarrassed. The camp director's daughter, the natural hiker, could not even get to the top of the hill without stopping everyone. As difficult as it was to do so, I had to accept the disheartening fact that I was not the fastest hiker on this trip.

I ended up being very discouraged that day because the most important thing to me was what other people thought about who I was. I had tied my identity too closely to something I did or didn't do. Whenever I place my identity in things I have to measure up to or things that change, God has a way of stopping me—literally this time—in my tracks. But only when I have come to a complete halt am I reminded of who I really am—God's beloved daughter. That's when God's words about Jesus come to me: "You are my beloved Son; with you I am well pleased" (Luke 3:22, ESV).

## "Stop! Everyone, stop! Johannah can't breathe!"

Because of Jesus, God is also pleased with me. I imagine God smiling when he thinks of me because he likes me just the way I am.

I am lovable not because I am a fast hiker or wear the funkiest pants. I am lovable simply because God made me, and I am his.

*Johannah Helen Wetzel*

# WHEN GOD
## breaks through

How do you answer the question "Who am I"? If we're really honest many of us might answer that question based on what we have, the people we know, or what others tell us about our status. "You're so smart!" "You are beautiful!" "Wow, you have the coolest clothes." Based on their feedback, we chase after whatever makes us worthy in their eyes, just as Johannah did. Gotta maintain status quo, right? But these opinions are based on ever-changing viewpoints.

The writer of Ecclesiastes, who understood the struggle for approval, commented, "I learned firsthand that pursuing all this is like chasing the wind" (Ecclesiastes 1:17, NLT). Tired of chasing after the wind? Consider a truth Johannah discovered, which the apostle Paul describes in his letter to the Ephesians:

> *When you believed in Christ, he identified you as his own by giving you the Holy Spirit, whom he promised long ago. The Spirit is God's guarantee that he will give us the inheritance he promised and that he has purchased us to be his own people (Ephesians 1:13–14, NLT).*

Your status with God will never change. It's not based on feelings or circumstances, achievements or possessions. Instead it has everything to do with God's love for you.

## my
## CHALLENGE

If you're wondering about the benefits of your status with God, check out the following Scriptures: John 1:12, 3:16; Romans 8:18–25, 31–39. In your journal, write what these verses mean to you.

# GOD IN THE BULLRING 35

## knowing **YOU** are not alone

A chorus of trumpets blared through the stands. Tambourines and drums echoed around the packed stadium, pumping excitement into the crowd. Glaring sun highlighted the dusty pit below.

Along with 50 other students, I had arrived in Ecuador to study for nine months at a Bible college. I still couldn't believe I was there! We planned to sightsee as much as possible. I gripped my greasy paper bag full of sweet pastries and sat back, ready to cheer the next man brave enough to challenge the vicious bull in this traditional Latin American event, the bullfight.

But as the day unfolded, I slowly became more and more skeptical of this event. Not just one man was in the bullring at a time, but a crowd of eager men, all seemingly oblivious to the danger they were in. I knew little about bullfighting, but none of them appeared to have any training in the "art." After witnessing several near-death incidents, I began to feel uncomfortable. I didn't want to support, or even watch, foolish men risk their lives for a good time. I was ready to leave. I headed down the stairs.

Then a woman shrieked loudly and I snapped my head back toward the bullring. My friend Erik had jumped into the bullring and was running close—too close—to the bull.

"Erik is going to try to touch the bull!" one of my friends yelled.

Erik lived according to the "I'll try anything once" principle, but I thought he would limit his daring escapades to eating raw fish, free-fall rock climbing, or maybe an occasional bungee jump. Shocked, I watched him face an angry bull.

The bull slammed Erik to the ground before he could even touch it. Erik tried to climb to his feet, but the bull scooped him up with its head and horns and flipped him to the ground a second time. The bull trampled and gored Erik's leg before Erik finally staggered out of the ring.

*"Erik!"* I screamed and ran to him.

I found him sprawled in the dust with a huge crowd gathered around him. I tried to get to him, but the crowd was too thick, and the police were backing everyone away. I pushed through the crowd; I had to see

**He's going to die. Please, God, don't let him die.**

Erik's face. A police officer angrily shoved me back, but then he saw Erik's hand reaching for mine. I gripped Erik's hand and fell to my knees beside him. His face was colorless and his left pant leg dripped with blood. A shiver ran down my back.

*He's going to die. Please, God, don't let him die.*

I persuaded someone to drive us to the hospital. In the car I stroked Erik's hair and held his leg up; my palms soon were covered with blood. I could barely keep from screaming and crying.

At the emergency entrance of the hospital, nurses surrounded the car. Erik was carried in on a board and doctors exchanged alarmed looks. Erik was wheeled into a room marked Critical, and I was sent to the lobby to wait.

As time passed I felt helpless, but called out to God in prayer, begging him to spare Erik's life. The Lord comforted my heart by reminding me of his promise in Psalm 139:16: "Every day of my life was recorded in your book. Every moment was laid out before a single day had passed" (NLT).

Erik's act was foolish, but God was in total control. I recalled Romans 8:38–39: "For I am convinced that neither death nor life, neither angels nor demons, neither the present nor the future, nor any powers, neither height nor depth, nor anything else in all creation, will be able to separate us from the love of God that is in Christ Jesus our Lord" (NIV). I breathed deeply, certain that God would not abandon Erik now. I reevaluated how I wanted to live my own life.

Moments later a nurse entered through the swinging doors with a report on Erik's condition. He would have permanent scars from the cuts, and the muscle damage in his leg was so severe that he might not be able to walk again, but he would be OK.

I sighed with relief—Erik would be OK!

Months passed as Erik slowly regained his strength. He went from bed rest and using a cane to hobble to finally walking on his own.

The world seems a little scarier almost every day—wars and calamities and poverty and terror. But day by day I'm learning to trust more deeply in God's promise never to leave us. I'm trying hard not to take my relationships for granted; I tell my family and friends more often that I love them. With God's help I'm learning that each day is a special gift and I must make the most of it—no matter what.

But I don't think I'll ever go to another bullfight.

*Allison Asimakoupoulos*

## WHEN GOD
### breaks through

Living in a foreign country, watching a close friend in great pain, and feeling totally helpless had to be a terrifying experience for Allison. Yet in her fears, Allison clung to one promise: God was with her; he was with Erik; and no matter what the outcome, he would not leave them. Sometimes we might feel we are all alone in a difficult situation with no one there to help us. When we have those feelings, we need to remember Jesus' final words to his disciples before he returned to heaven: "And be sure of this: I am with you always, even to the end of the age" (Matthew 28:20, NLT). He may not be with us physically, but Jesus is with us through the gift of the Holy Spirit. Jesus' promise is for all times, to all people who profess their faith in him. You are not alone.

### my
## CHALLENGE

Think of something you could carry with you (such as a coin or a small card), or wear (like a ring or a wristband) that will help you remember Jesus' words in Matthew 28:20. Or write Jesus' promise on an index card and place it where you will see it every morning before you leave for school. Remind yourself each time you leave home that Jesus is with you.

MAKING PLANS 36

## learning to **COOPERATE** with God

Rejected! How could this happen to me? I thought I had found the perfect college and the school where God wanted me to be.

I had expected my junior year of high school to be stressful, with difficult classes, the ACT, and the search for the perfect college. I didn't really know where I wanted to go to college, but I felt I had plenty of time to decide. Our local community college was definitely out; I was sure of that much. I took the ACT twice. I was happy when my junior year ended and I became a senior. Now I could be lazy and life would not be so stressful. Or so I thought.

In October of my senior year, I took a road trip with my best friend, Emily, and our moms to visit Indiana Wesleyan and Taylor University. Both schools were nice, but as I walked around the campuses I felt that I did not belong at either school. The next weekend I visited Moody Bible Institute, where another good friend, Bekah, attended.

I had found the perfect college! The students were great, the professors were amazing, and what better location than Chicago. I knew then that Moody was where I wanted to be, and that God wanted me there too.

So on to the next step of the process—applications. This was more stressful than I had ever imagined! I decided to apply to Indiana Wesleyan and Moody. The Moody application had six essay questions and required three recommendation letters. The application took me two months to fill out, but I managed to make the early decision deadline. I also sent my Indiana Wesleyan application. Now I could only wait.

Waiting was definitely one of the hardest things I have ever done! While I was waiting, I prayed daily about Moody. The chance of getting into Moody was slim—only 30 percent. But I believed God wanted me there and that I would get in.

Finally a letter came from Indiana Wesleyan—I had been accepted! This was a great relief. One down, one to go.

On January 16, the letter from Moody arrived. I was terrified to open it. I uttered one last prayer to God, ripped the envelope open, and began to read. *We regret to inform you that your application has not been accepted at this time.* Completely shocked, I finished the letter, set it down, and began to sob.

**We regret to inform you that your application has not been accepted at this time.**

My mom tried to talk to me about Indiana Wesleyan, but I was not ready to accept that I had been rejected by Moody. When I told Bekah that I was rejected, she quoted Jeremiah 29:11: "'For I know the plans I have for you,' says the LORD. 'They are plans for good and not for disaster, to give you a future and a hope'" (NLT). God told this to the Jews who were exiled to Babylon and didn't know what to do. This helped some, but it wasn't something I really wanted to hear.

When I went to school the next day, the word "rejected" filled my mind. It was hard to focus on other things. I told only one of my friends that day, trying hard not to cry. She gave me a hug and said she was sorry, but I couldn't tell my other friends for fear I *would* cry and I didn't want to admit to myself that I truly had been rejected.

I can't really pinpoint the moment I became OK with it, but I began to accept the rejection. This wouldn't be the end of the world, and if God wanted me at Moody, I would get there. Right now God seemed to have other plans for me. Prayer helped a lot. I prayed constantly about accepting my situation, and I asked others—friends, my small group, and my parents—to pray for me too.

Eventually I decided against going to Indiana Wesleyan and chose the community college I had been dead set against! I am taking many of my general education courses now and will apply again to Moody as a transfer student. Transfers are supposed to get in more easily, but I will once again have to wait and see. I guess God must want me to work on my patience!

I am still learning to accept that I'm at home while all of my friends have gone off to college. But I know God has a good plan for my life, and that fills me with hope.

*Marija Birchard*

# WHEN GOD
## breaks through

No one likes to feel rejected. Rejection erodes self-esteem and confidence. It causes us to second-guess ourselves and God as we struggle to shift plans. Sometimes we fall prey to feelings of anger, sadness, betrayal, or resentment. Like Marija, we can know that God can still work in us even through the bitterness of rejection.

Plans, like seasons, frequently change. "We can make our plans, but the LORD determines our steps" (Proverbs 16:9, NLT). The sovereign God has the final say over any plans. While we may be tempted to believe that rejection is the end of our plans, God may say otherwise. That's why we need to practice patience and perseverance. God's "no" might just mean "no for now."

## my
## CHALLENGE

Consider some plans or decisions you've made recently. Are you willing to accept God's answers, even if they're "no" or "wait"? If you feel discouraged because of a rejection, consider these words from Philippians: "I am certain that God, who began the good work within you, will continue his work until it is finally finished on the day when Christ Jesus returns" (Philippians 1:6, NLT).

## overcoming **BULIMIA**

Stomping out of the house, I heard the door slam behind me. Still fuming, I drove away and pulled into a park nearby. *Only one thing will relieve my tension,* I thought. Kneeling on the grass I looked like I was praying, praying for God to heal the hurt between my mom and me. But anger blocked me from praying. Leaning over, I stuck my finger down my throat and forced myself to throw up.

Vomiting had become a familiar ritual, and that was scary. Sitting back, I pushed strands of hair off my damp face, spitting the bitter taste from my mouth. Although overwhelmed with relief, I also felt ashamed. *Why am I doing this?* I wondered. It seemed that the only way to handle the intensity of my emotion was to eat and throw up. I knew the name for my behavior, but I denied it for a long time. Desperation was beginning to overwhelm me. As the night air closed in and I sat alone on the grass looking around the abandoned park, I finally admitted it: *I am bulimic.*

The next day the sun woke me early, too early to call the church for counseling. I got in the shower and debated what to do.

*Maybe things will get better,* I told myself. *If I try really hard, I think I can handle this. I just need to stop doing it.*

The lie sat heavily on my heart. This would not get better on its own and I knew it, having already tried and tried. As the water chilled I reached for my towel and wrapped myself in its comforting warmth.

Taking a deep breath I picked up the phone. The church receptionist

answered and asked how she could help. My resolve nearly vanished. Feeling the familiar shame I thought, *I lead a ministry at my school, have lots of friends, and make good grades. I do not need a counselor.*

I was tempted to hang up, but the words "I need a counselor" tumbled from my mouth. Without comment, the receptionist kindly gave me a name and phone number. I made one more call.

With patience, kindness, and wisdom, my therapist, Caroline, led me deeply into the pain, and we began to explore the hurt that had infused my life for so long.

An abiding fear of punishment ruled my life. Fueled by a legalistic religious upbringing and a punitive father, I was terrified of God and my dad. As a result I became "the perfect little girl." Even though I tried to do everything right, I still lived in fear, knowing my father's wrath was arbitrary and worrying that God would damn me to hell.

One day Caroline asked, "Who is Jesus to you?" The question irritated me. I'd known Jesus a long time, I'd introduced him to others, and I always led a good, moral life. I began, "Well, he's God; he loves me; he died for me—"

Caroline's eyes locked on mine as she gently interrupted. "No, no, Jeanine. Who is Jesus *to you?*"

Her gaze did not waiver, and I knew that correctly understanding the Bible would not work here; Caroline was appealing to my heart. The chasm between my heart and mind was wide and deep and not easily bridged. It was safe and easy to believe in my head that Jesus loved me. But to let his love enter my heart was too risky. *Besides, if he really loved me, my life wouldn't be such a mess,* I'd determined.

**An abiding fear of punishment ruled my life.**

With a sigh, I shook my head. "Oh, Caroline, Jesus doesn't really care about me. I guess I *know* he cares about me, but I don't *feel* that way. Why would he let all these things happen in my life if he really loves me?"

The tears finally slid down my cheeks. Now I was angry. Caroline didn't offer any answers to my question, but tears dripped down her cheeks too. Our session ended and tissue in hand, I walked out the door.

Something inside me had shifted. I began to feel my anger and articulate it. Many nights, with tears and rage, I challenged Jesus to reveal his love to me. Mom and I started to talk and work on healing the rift between us. The irrational fear that had dominated my life began to diminish. Failure still evoked shame, but I gave myself the space to be imperfect. My need to binge and purge lessened.

Caroline and I met weekly for three years, talking and crying together. It was hard work, but if I was to find Jesus, really find him, I had to work on building the bridge that would connect my heart and mind. Knowing all the right answers was no longer enough; I wanted to *experience* them. The truth in my head needed to become the truth in my heart.

One cold, wintry day, as I sat across from Caroline, something unexpected happened. As I recounted a painful memory, it was as if Caroline faded away and I saw Jesus through her. In that moment I realized: *Caroline loves me, listens to me, and offers her faith when I have none. She is Jesus to me.*

Caroline loves me because Jesus loves her. His love enables her to give so much to me; it is not so much her love as it is his. Sitting quietly I looked inside myself. Surprisingly I saw Jesus, tenderly and quietly building the bridge alongside me as committed to my healing as I was. He wanted the truth of who he was to live in my heart as much as I did. And enough of the bridge is finished that today I finally know he loves me.

I know it in my head *and* in my heart.

*Jeanine Pynes*

# WHEN GOD
## breaks through

One day on a dusty road, Jesus asked his followers the same question Jeanine's counselor asked her.

> Jesus and his disciples left Galilee and went up to the villages near Caesarea Philippi. As they were walking along, he asked them, "Who do people say I am?"
>
> "Well," they replied, "some say John the Baptist, some say Elijah, and others say you are one of the other prophets."
>
> Then he asked them, "But who do you say I am?"
>
> Peter replied, "You are the Messiah" (Mark 8:27–29, NLT).

Sadly, just a few verses away, Jesus had to rebuke the man who spoke such stirring words about his messiahship!

Sometimes our head knowledge doesn't match our heart knowledge. It takes a hard circumstance to show us what we really believe about God. At a time like that, we might cling to platitudes or live in denial, covering over our hurts—at least until God rips the scab off the wounds. He doesn't do this to harm, but to heal—to take us beyond parroted beliefs to those that rend the heart and cut to the bone.

## my
## CHALLENGE

Who is Jesus to you? If you journal, take a moment to write a description of him. Don't just use your head. Use your heart as you think of who or what he is to you.

## reaching out **INSTEAD** of judging

I disliked Josh from the first day I met him when he sat next to me in French class my sophomore year. Short, stocky, and extremely chiseled, Josh seemed rough around the edges and too self-involved. He used too much foul language. One of my first thoughts about him was that I was pretty sure he would never believe in Jesus. Besides he was only interested in one thing: wrestling.

I had never liked or understood wrestling—why anyone would want to roll around on gross gym mats in spandex suits was completely beyond me. But Josh loved wrestling. He wore T-shirts promoting wrestling, he talked about his lifting schedule, and he openly shared how much weight he was trying to gain or lose each week. I was convinced we were nothing alike.

I planned simply to ignore him, and my plan worked—mostly. I talked to the other people around me before and after class, and Josh got the picture quickly. But instead of ignoring me, he tried even harder to get my attention. It drove me nuts! I didn't want to get to know him, I didn't want to be his friend, and I didn't want to hear about wrestling!

The following year Josh and I were in the same French class again. Upperclassmen could choose seats so on the first day of class I sat on the far side of the room. When Josh walked in I looked down and focused on my flip-flops, but Josh plopped down in the seat next to mine.

"Hey, Ann! I think it'd be fun to sit next to each other again this year, don't you?"

I looked at him, trying to force a grin. "Uh . . . sure." There was an awkward pause. I couldn't stand the silence. "How was your summer?"

"Sweet. I worked for my dad's construction company in the mornings and spent almost three hours every day lifting and running for wrestling."

*Oh no. More never-ending conversations about wrestling!*

"I think I can make it to the state tournament this year," Josh went on, "and I'm really stoked about it. I'm gonna be training all the time."

I wondered if he could talk about other sports. "I'm on the volleyball team this year," I said. "I think we might have a chance to make it to the state tournament too."

**Maybe I had been wrong about Josh.**

"Really?" Josh looked interested. "That's awesome! I'll definitely make it to some of your games." I looked at him warily, but he insisted. "No, really—I'll come to your first game. When is it?"

"Next week, Tuesday night."

"OK. I'll be there. You gotta win, OK?" He offered me a high five, and I couldn't help but smile.

Our teacher started class, but I was distracted most of the hour. Maybe I had been wrong about Josh.

On Tuesday night Josh came to the game and stayed for the whole match. I thanked him in class the next morning for making the time to be at the game.

"I enjoyed it," he said. "I'll be there again."

And he was. Josh became one of our team's most loyal supporters, and Josh and I became friends. Before long I began to genuinely care about Josh, especially when I discovered that although he had heard about Jesus, he had never made a decision about him. Jesus had stepped into my life a couple of years before high school, giving me more joy and hope than I had ever experienced and I wanted Josh to come to faith too. So when Josh actually made it to the state wrestling tournament in February, I took a risk and gave him a gift—a Bible. I attached a note with it:

*Josh,*

*Good luck on going to the state tournament! I know you've worked really hard to make it this far and it's been great to see you do so well. I was trying to think of a good gift to get you and this is the best thing I could ever give to you. We've talked about what it means to be a Christian, and I want to give you this Bible because reading the Bible and believing in Christ have changed my life. Jesus has given me more hope and joy than I ever thought possible. I marked some of my favorite verses in your Bible and I hope you will read them. If you ever want to talk about this stuff, I'd love to talk with you.*

*Ann*

I wasn't sure how he would react to the gift, but I gave it to him one afternoon as we were leaving class. When I saw him the next day, he gave me a hug, squeezing me with his huge arms.

"Ann, thanks so much for the Bible! I really appreciate it."

"Really? To be honest I wasn't sure if you'd like it or not." I paused. "But I meant what I wrote, Josh. Jesus has saved my life and he's given me real hope and joy."

Josh nodded. "I can tell, Ann. You've always been really joyful. That's why I wanted to be your friend, even when you tried to ignore me all last year."

"You noticed?" I felt my face redden. "I'm so sorry—I, I just didn't know you, that's all." I looked at the ground and tried to find courage. "Josh, would you want to go to church with me on Sunday?"

He hesitated. "Maybe. The state tournament starts on Tuesday, but—maybe I could make it."

Josh didn't come to church that Sunday and he didn't win the state tournament that year. But he came to church the following Sunday . . . and the next . . . and the next. And that summer Josh gave his life to Jesus. With the help and encouragement of our youth pastor and others in the youth group, he started living for Christ and his joy was contagious. He couldn't stop talking about Jesus and how Christ had saved and changed his life.

During our senior year Josh *did* win a state wrestling title and he did so much more than that—he led his younger brother to faith in Jesus. Now Josh is living in the inner city of Philadelphia serving as a missionary there.

When I met Josh, I never imagined he would become a man of God, living for Christ's glory. But that was because I was seeing with my own eyes, not God's. Now when I start judging others, I think of Josh and try to love them instead, knowing that God is able to change anyone's heart and life!

*Ann Swindell*

## WHEN GOD
### breaks through

Ann had spent a whole year judging Josh, focusing on his faults and quirks instead of trying to see him as God sees him. Does that sound familiar? Sadly our "default" mode is "judging," rather than "loving" or "encouraging." In the Gospel of Matthew, Jesus reminds us of his call to love others rather than judge them: "Do not judge, or you too will be judged. For in the same way you judge others, you will be judged, and with the measure you use, it will be measured to you. "Why do you look at the speck of sawdust in your brother's eye and pay no attention to the plank in your own eye" (Matthew 7:1-3, NIV)?

my
## CHALLENGE

Do you automatically judge someone? Consider praying for that person or writing him or her a note of encouragement just as Ann did for Josh.

## appreciating the **COMMUNITY** of believers

That first Christmas without Uncle Scott, I watched my grandmother cry.

Her jubilant facade quivered as her heart overflowed. She had held her own better than most; she sat through the excitement as we younger grandchildren exuberantly tore open packages, and she even opened a few of her own. But after all the ruckus of Christmas morning died down, the light, gentle sobs of a resigned old woman caught me in midsentence.

Here, in my aunt's cozy Colorado home, a thousand miles away from my grandmother's house where we usually celebrated Christmas, the pangs of grief were still present. Grandmother wiped blurred eyes behind her glasses and I could only hope my own emotional fortifications would hold.

A week later, while enjoying New Year's Eve with my other set of relatives, I saw my aunt cry. We'd been watching old, forgotten home movies that had been converted into DVDs. From the screen my cousin Beth—my aunt's daughter—waved, expressed her hopes and wishes for the future, dressed her brother in ridiculous outfits, and talked to her mom.

As a new scene started, I saw my aunt's jaw quiver. She was trying so hard to hold back the flood of emotions that her eyes reddened. It was futile though, as a tear began to trace its way down my aunt's cheek, and again I felt the sobering effect on my heart.

I didn't cry either of those days. I had grieved those deaths and was all cried out. Still I felt guilty as both mothers mourned their dead children. Scott, my uncle, had died during the year, while Beth, my eight-year-old cousin, had died 10 years earlier. No matter when their deaths had occurred, though, their memories penetrated my grandmother's and aunt's minds.

I didn't want the spectator role. I remembered a time, six months earlier when, after promising not to cry, I delivered a sobbing wreck of a poetic eulogy for my uncle. Had it not been for the comforting hug I received as words poured from my mouth and brought pungent memories to the surface of my mind, I would never have known the sweetness that can come in mourning. The community I felt at that moment was the rose at the end of all those thorns. I saw that rose bloom when I grieved for my uncle, and I saw it bloom when as a five-year-old, I watched my aunt surrounded by praying family and friends.

> **The community I felt at that moment was the rose at the end of all those thorns.**

I didn't have an epiphany at that moment—just a nudge from the Holy Spirit, an observation of a time when my soul flooded beyond capacity. My rivers of emotions remained in check, but I rose and embraced each of my grief-weary relations.

All at once I knew that if Scott and Beth were there, they would have done the same thing, because God doesn't want us to go through life alone.

*Justin Hanselman*

## WHEN GOD
### breaks through

Grief is the great divider, an emotion that locks us away from each other. We're embarrassed to admit how much we hurt. But as Justin determined, we need each other. The apostle Paul described community this way: "A body is made up of many parts, and each of them has its own use. That's how it is with us. There are many of us, but we each are part of the body of Christ, as well as part of one another. . . . When others are happy, be happy with them, and when they are sad, be sad" (Romans 12:4–5, 15, cev).

### my
## CHALLENGE

Who can you rejoice with today? Send that person an IM or an e-mail celebrating his or her good news. Or do you know someone who is sad right now? Spend a few moments praying for him or her. Let that person know you have been thinking and praying for him or her.

# TAKING THE HEAT 40

## watching God **WORK** in difficult times

The firefighter said it was their nightmare kind of day: very dry, windy, and in the middle of a drought. I wish we'd thought about that earlier—before flames were shooting over treetops and approaching $800,000 homes. But I'm getting ahead of myself.

What's a good World War II epic movie without special effects? My friends and I asked ourselves this before we filmed a friend's history project. This wasn't our first movie together. We loved choosing the stories, props, costumes, and location, and storyboarding all the shots. A group of us had even gone to film camp together and worked on a real movie set. Despite that sometimes we chose action shots that involved a little risky behavior, but nothing bad had ever happened.

That day in March would be "a day that will live in infamy," as President Franklin Delano Roosevelt once said.

A group of us met in the woods and the shooting was going well. We had lots of footage of battle scenes, secret attacks, and actors dressed in camouflage throwing grenades. We were in the middle of a scene where a minor character met his demise trying to take the enemy by surprise. Suddenly one of the firecrackers we were using as a fake explosive shot up into the air and landed in the crispy brush.

It truly only takes a spark to get a fire going. The sparks fell into the leaves and instantly combusted. The flames quickly spread to the surrounding brush, then to a dry pine tree and then it seemed the whole world was on fire.

The moment of truth came when the fire grew so far out of control that we each had to make a decision: Do I run and hide and pretend I wasn't involved? Or do I stay and take the heat? If I ran quickly maybe no one would ever know I was involved. But what if the fire injured someone? What if someone's house burned down?

Along the way in my life, God had taught me that being a noble man meant taking responsibility for my choices, mistakes, and actions. This was my moment of truth. Had I learned that lesson?

At just that moment half of our group did what I contemplated doing—they took off for home. I thought again about the consequences as we tried to beat down the flames one last time. One of my friends stripped to his underwear, using his clothes to try to smother the blaze. Finally realizing it was futile and that we were approaching a major forest fire, I grabbed the three guys I was with, pulled them into a huddle and said a quick prayer. Then I ran for help.

**Do I run and hide and pretend I wasn't involved? Or do I stay and take the heat?**

Thankfully, when I got down the road, someone had already called the fire department and a fire chief met me on the edge of the road, leaning on his car and chewing tobacco. "You guys responsible for this?" he asked.

"Yup," I panted, out of breath from running.

"Go over there and talk to the fire marshal," he said.

Next the police arrived. They weren't as calm as the chief. Fire trucks came next, including four-wheel drive vehicles borrowed from the U.S. Department of Forestry to handle the wooded terrain. Helicopters arrived, picking up water from a nearby lake to dump on the fire. We were told to call our parents. When my dad arrived, the rescue workers sent us home because the area wasn't safe.

On the evening news they showed people in the nearby houses moving their pictures and valuables out of their homes because the fire smoldered at the edge of their property. High winds and dry conditions frustrated firefighters' efforts to stop the blaze, so it raged well into the night. They kept watch, trying to get it under control and keep the hot spots from flaming up again. The wind finally died down. In the end 17 acres of woods burned. Once the fire was out, the rain arrived.

The amazing part of the story is that we lived in a congested suburb. Yet the fire stayed on the few areas of unoccupied land and never touched a piece of private property, never crossed a property line, and never harmed a person. If you saw the bustling suburban area where the fire took place, you'd know that God intervened that day.

Most of the guys involved weren't believers. The next day they talked about the irony of the rain coming *after* the fire was out. I knew the timing didn't mean that God wasn't in control. If the fire had never started or if it had been a tiny brush fire that we could've put out ourselves, I never would have seen how God is in control of everything. He took a terrible situation and protected us by commanding the flames. Most importantly I learned that God doesn't always take us out of the fires of life, but he definitely walks through them with us. Because of his mercy and protection, I'll think more before I make another decision about movies, life, relationships—and exploding special effects.

*Jamison M. as told to Linda MacKillop*

## WHEN GOD
### breaks through

God doesn't always take us out of a hot situation. Sometimes he leaves us there to assure us of his presence. Shadrach, Meshach, and Abednego, three guys from Israel, ended up in a fiery situation of their own. They chose not to worship the huge idol set up in Babylon. (Read Daniel 3.) Their loyalty to God earned them a death sentence in a furnace. Although God vetoed the execution order, they still went in the furnace for a time. But he went with them.

### my
## CHALLENGE

Feeling the slow burn of a current or past mistake? Check out Isaiah 43:2: "When you walk through the fire of oppression, you will not be burned up; the flames will not consume you." How does this promise make you feel?

# TAKING THE HIGH ROAD 41

## learning to **RELY** on God

We were filthy. We had not been clean in almost two weeks. We smelled so badly we had to turn away from ourselves. Getting out of my sleeping bag in the mornings was a test of speed and lung capacity. I would hold my breath because as I opened my bag the smell of me that had been cooped up inside the bag all night would be set free. I would race to get to clean air.

I was on Highroad.

My siblings and I each celebrated college graduation by giving ourselves a gift of some sort. My oldest brother took a 900-mile canoe trip down the Yukon River in Alaska. The next oldest went to Switzerland. My sister bought herself a car. I decided that torture would be a good way to start adulthood and signed up for Highroad.

That was one of the best decisions of my life.

Highroad is a wilderness camping/hiking journey in Northern Wisconsin. By going on this trip I was removing from my life the things I depended on most. No cars. No TV. No phones. No radios. No computers. No running water.

We had absolutely no communication with the outside world. My group saw no one for days. We didn't have a couch to be a potato on. No comfy bed at the end of a long day. You relied on those traveling with you, just as they relied on you. And you were forced to rely on God.

More than a dozen men and women I didn't know and I set out with our 40- to 60-pound packs. Each day the leaders pointed to a place on the map and told us to get there by nightfall. Once we reached our destination we boiled water and ate a surprise air-packaged dinner before bedding down for the night.

Some days went very well. We found the trail with no problem and got into camp with daylight to spare. Once we even came upon a natural spring and didn't have to boil our water—it was a gift.

Other days were not quite as smooth. On those days we didn't find the trail. Or we were on the wrong trail and the only way to reach the correct one was to travel straight through the woods, using only our compass and maps to be sure we were headed right.

On those days bushwhacking with a compass was how we found our way. (For wilderness novices, bushwhacking is creating a path through the woods and brush by moving or chopping down whatever is in front of you.) That took extra time and energy. It hurt more, was never easy, and we were often uncertain about our destination until we were actually there.

**You were forced to rely on God.**

One afternoon we bushwhacked ourselves into a river that seemed uncrossable. By God's grace we found a beaver's dam strong enough to hold each of us and our packs. One by one we unhooked our waist belts (in case we fell in the river) and slowly crossed to the other side. We all made it over dry and continued our bushwhacking.

In the end we made it back to camp safely. The evening of our return we showered and met at the dining hall. Back in camp I quickly realized how much I'd come to love the silence of the woods and depending on God and those around me.

*Margaret Henry*

# WHEN GOD
## breaks through

On what do you rely? It depends on the circumstances, doesn't it? If we need direction we might rely on a variety of resources: GPS, Google maps, or the advice of others. If we need entertainment we rely on the radio, iPod, cell phone, or computer. But when the power goes down, all of these things prove unreliable.

During Margaret's Highroad experience she learned to rely on God to keep her team on the right paths. She had no other resource. David, an Old Testament king and psalm writer came to the same realization as he explained in two psalms. "You have made a wide path for my feet to keep them from slipping," (Psalm 18:36, NLT). "Your word is a lamp to guide my feet and a light for my path" (Psalm 119:105, NLT). Reading God's Word and communicating with him through prayer helped David (and Margaret) feel assured and confident. Both knew God could keep them from slipping—making a wrong choice.

Stress comes when we aren't sure where we're going or how to get from point A to point B. When you need guidance turn to the ultimate "GPS" system: God, Prayer, and Scriptures.

## my
## CHALLENGE

What are the resources (people or things) you turn to when you need direction? Which is most reliable? Why? If you didn't have that resource, what would you do? How would your life change if you used "the ultimate GPS system" for guidance in every decision?

153

## meeting the God who **SEES** all

Jesus invaded my life on the night I decided I was going to die. I was 14 and desperately lonely. My dad had walked out on my mom, my little brother, and me two years earlier. For these two years I partied and wondered why my dad had left me. The pain led to this point—me sitting on my bed holding a bottle of vodka and staring at the pills I had lined up on my desk.

This was it. I was ending the pain once and for all.

As the tears streamed down my face, I realized I had gone to school for the last time. I had hugged my little brother for the last time and spoken to my mom for the last time.

Life is filled with last times, but most people never realize those moments when they are in them. I was actually relieved, realizing that these were my last minutes of pain. No more fights with friends, cramming for tests, hoping some guy would look at me. No more Friday night parties or Saturday hangovers or wishing I looked like the models in the magazines.

I hadn't always been in this much pain. Alcohol helped me push down the pain for quite awhile. Escaping into a bottle was what I had lived for these past two years.

Even after multiple blackouts I still couldn't find anything that helped me more than alcohol.

I tried to stop drinking. I would clean up my act for a few days, but the hurt always came back. I even tried to find out about God. I went to a youth group to see if they knew how to help me. The people were nice and I enjoyed the time with them, but the God they talked about felt so far away. How could that God understand me? How could he ever help me when I couldn't even help myself? Why should he care about my life when the world was filled with other problems? I liked the idea of being able to know a God that big, but it seemed impossible. He was so far away.

One night one of the youth leaders told me she was praying for me. The idea of someone talking to God about me made me feel loved. But it wasn't enough to keep me from drinking. I worked hard to become friends with older kids who could get booze for me. Life was too scary to face it alone. I felt hopeless.

Twice I nearly died of alcohol poisoning. Early one Saturday morning my mom walked into my room and found me unconscious. Two days later I woke up in the psych ward at the hospital. The counselors said I couldn't leave until I let them help me.

I went to all the group therapy sessions and said everything I thought the counselors wanted to hear. I was polite and promised to stop drinking. I apologized to my mom. On the outside I looked like I would be OK. However inside I was desperate to find something to ease the pain. I felt unloved and alone.

**Two days later I woke up in the psych ward at the hospital.**

*I wonder what happens after you die,* I thought as I sat on the bed contemplating the pills.

I tried to convince my favorite teddy bear that even though I was probably going to hell, it wouldn't be as bad as my life was.

For the first time ever, I called out to God. "God, I am not even sure if you see me here, but I want you to understand that I can't go on living like this. I know killing myself is wrong, but you have to understand—my dad left me. He just walked out and I haven't heard a word from him in two years.

"God, I wish you could have done something for me. I know it's a lot to ask, but I wish you could have brought my dad back. That would have made a big difference. I didn't expect him to move back in. It just would have been nice if sometime in the past two years, you could have had him show up or call me. But now it's too late."

Suddenly my phone rang. At first I ignored it, but then I glanced at the pills and realized this would be the last person I would ever talk to. It was probably one of my friends; for some reason I needed to hear one last voice.

"Amber, are you there?"

"Dad!" I choked out. "Dad, is that you?"

"Yes, honey, it's me. How are you?"

I could hardly speak. "Dad, how did you know to call me?"

My dad sounded puzzled, "I just miss you so much and have been too ashamed to call. But tonight I felt like I had to try. I dialed your number several times and then was so scared I hung up. But something made me keep trying."

I couldn't believe it. Of all the nights to call me, how did he know I needed to hear from him then?

I couldn't hold it in any longer. I told my dad everything. How hurt I was, how mad and lonely I was. Most importantly I told him about the pills and my decision to end it all that night.

When I took a breath, I realized my dad was crying. He told me he would be right over. "Amber, please don't do anything. Please wait for me to get there."

I lay on my bed and tried to comprehend the miracle that had just happened. God had heard me; he brought my dad to me. Maybe it was possible to be loved and known by this big powerful God. I tried to remember what else I had heard. What had people at church said about a relationship with Jesus? I couldn't remember exactly, but I knew I had to go back there and find out.

For the first time in years, I felt peaceful. My dad was on his way, I didn't have to die, God actually knew who I was. Maybe God wasn't as far away as he seemed.

Three days later I walked back into that youth group. The staff was happy to see me. One of them sat down with me that night (and many following nights) and listened as I poured out my heart. I told her about my family, my drinking, the psych ward, and the night I almost killed myself. More importantly, I asked questions about life and Jesus.

I finally surrendered my life to Jesus one month after I nearly surrendered to pills and vodka. My life didn't become perfect. My parents still divorced, I struggled to let go of the alcohol, and I lost many of the people I thought were my friends. However the peace and joy that Jesus brought helped me face my problems.

I realized I really did die that night. The old Amber who felt unloved and worthless died and the new Amber was born—an Amber who knows she is loved by God.

*Amber M. as told to Nina Edwards*

## WHEN GOD
### breaks through

Hagar, a woman living during Old Testament times, thought life was over for her more than once. In despair she ran away (Genesis 16). After returning to the same sad situation, she was later forced away (Genesis 21). During both experiences the God who seemed far away met her. Because of her experience Hagar had a new name for God: "Thereafter, Hagar used another name to refer to the LORD, who had spoken to her. She said, 'You are the God who sees me.' She also said, 'Have I truly seen the One who sees me?' " (Genesis 16:13, NLT).

### my
## CHALLENGE

Perhaps like Amber you're wondering if you have the courage to continue. If so, like Amber you can cry out to "the God who sees you." Even if you find it difficult to believe he cares, he does.

Hagar called God "the God who sees me." Based on your experience, what would you call God?

# AN EMBARRASSING 43 MOMENT

## putting God's **LOVE** to practical use

I never meant to strip in front of the school. But in a way, doing so led me to Jesus.

It had all started months earlier. "Listen up, ladies!" the coach yelled, trying to get all the girls' attention before the gym emptied. "Next Tuesday is the girl's basketball team tryouts. If you want to be on the team, this is your last chance to practice. We'll meet here every day next week after school. We will run drills and watch to see how well you do and we'll go from there. A list of who made the cut will be posted on the door by the following Monday afternoon."

An excited clamor filled the gym. Looking around I saw that most of the noise came from the girls in the popular crowd—the ones who were on the team every year.

I was not in the "in" crowd, nor did I want to be. At least that was the lie I told myself and my friends. I knew that the popular girls were flat-out mean to anyone who was different from them. They were, and only wanted to be, with their own cliques: the pretty ones, the jocks, and the partiers who had gobs of friends.

"Are you going to try out this year?" Natalie, my best friend, asked me.

"No." I shook my head. "I don't have any desire to humiliate myself. You know the same girls are always on the team, and I don't fit in with them."

"Karen seems to be different though," Natalie said, pushing her glasses up her nose. "You haven't changed your mind about her?"

"She *seems* to be different, but she's the main one of that clique. Come on, let's go." I pulled Natalie out of the gym and away, dropping the idea of

playing basketball from my dream list. Until Karen talked to me, that is.

Karen, the most popular girl in school, had it all. She was pretty, she was head cheerleader, and she had made All-American in *every* female sport. She was an honor student, president of everything that mattered in high school, and had all the boys drooling after her. Every girl dreamed of becoming Karen. But morphing into her was impossible, so they fought to be her best friend.

So when Karen approached me and asked, "Toni, why don't you try out for the basketball team?" I couldn't believe it.

"Me?"

"Yeah. Why not you? Try out. I'll be praying for you." She said this over her shoulder as she walked away.

I was shocked the girl even knew who I was! If I hadn't been watching Karen, I would have thought she was trying to win some cruel contest by getting me to go out for the basketball team. But I had observed her closely for a long time. I saw her interact with the teachers, her friends, and other students. I studied her when she didn't know I was looking. She was very different from the typical popular girl. She didn't seem to put on an act for anyone. She was the same no matter whom she was around.

"The worst thing I ever heard anyone say about her is that she lives like she thinks Jesus would want her to," I told Natalie.

"So are you going to try out now?" Natalie asked.

"Well, yeah! She's praying for me," I said, mocking Karen while trying to hide how thrilled I was at her invitation. "I simply *have* to try out now!"

I tried out and made the team! Karen seemed genuinely happy for me. At first I sat on the bench most of the time because once I got on the court with the ball I'd panic and shoot the ball straight up in the air. But as time went on I got better. My confidence grew every time Karen cheered me on. She even showed me drills to improve my skills.

One minute I was gaining self-assurance, the next moment it was stripped away. Literally.

We were playing our biggest game. Because the game started before school let out, the gym was filled with teachers, parents, and the entire student body.

Our school didn't have regular uniforms, so we wore a sleeveless vest (a penny) with the team name and number on it. Those pennies fit over our heads and over our blouses. When substitutions were made we would switch pennies.

At the end of the third quarter, the coach motioned me off the court while another girl ran to take my place. The clock was still ticking so I reached down, grabbed the bottom of my penny, pulled it over my head, and handed it to the other player.

Suddenly all the spectators in the gym were standing on their feet pointing.

"What?" I turned but didn't see what had the crowd so excited—until I felt the draft. I had not only taken the penny off, but also my blouse underneath it!

I was totally embarrassed and holding back tears while trying to untangle my blouse from the penny. I heard the crowd clearly now—most of them were singing the striptease song.

The rest were loudly catcalling until Karen stood between them and me. She quieted the gym without saying a word. Taking the tangled clothes from me, Karen quickly separated them, turned them right side out, and dressed me.

**I had not only taken the penny off, but also my blouse underneath it!**

In all my humiliation that day, no parent, teacher, coach, or friend came to my rescue. Only this girl, the most popular in the whole school, came to help me. Karen didn't calm a sea for me like the Bible story I had heard about when Jesus calmed a raging storm for the scared disciples, but she did quiet a sea of laughter. Her bold, compassionate action comforted me.

She never preached at me, but her reputation said everything. Her gentle ways demonstrated to me that God loved me.

I changed from being like all the other girls in school who wanted to *be* Karen, to wanting to be *like* Karen in showing Christ's love to someone else.

After that day I didn't worry so much about being in the "in" crowd. I wanted to live like Jesus wanted me to. I looked for opportunities to be a true friend and to pray for others, even out loud.

*Toni Peinado*

# WHEN GOD
## breaks through

Karen lived a truth the apostle Paul wrote about in Romans: "Don't just pretend to love others. Really love them. Hate what is wrong. Hold tightly to what is good" (Romans 12:9, NLT). He could write that because Jesus lived it and inspired Paul to live it too.

Jesus was the ultimate trendsetter, one who experienced the popularity and the derision of the crowd. But he kept his eyes on his Father instead of the crowd. Because of that, he could truly love others instead of his own reputation.

## my
## CHALLENGE

How can you put Paul's words into action this week?

# THE LIFTING 44

## defeating the **GIANTS** of life

"Excuse me. I don't know if you remember me. I'm Marylou."

I turned to see a familiar-looking girl with long dark hair standing in the hallway outside of my high school Spanish class. I struggled to remember where I had seen her before.

"Oh. Hi, Marylou," I said, trying to cover over my embarrassment. She was apparently more uncomfortable than I was. I smiled encouragingly.

Taking a deep breath she looked me in the eyes and seemed to find strength to continue. "I just wanted to say, um, sorry for the way we treated you. We were all kind of stupid then." She shifted her eyes to her feet.

"No problem, Marylou. Thanks," I said automatically, still unsure of what she was talking about.

Her face relaxed into an expression of relief and she smiled shyly. "Well, anyway, I see you are busy, so I will let you go."

As she hurried away the memory of elementary school and the endless days of fear and loneliness flooded back on me. It was some years back, but suddenly it felt like yesterday. We had just moved to La Puente, California, and I was a minority—one of the few Caucasians in a primarily Hispanic school where any difference was immediately pounced on. I was known as the *gringa* (white girl). Recess was a nightmare as I tried in vain to become invisible to the others.

I excelled in the classroom and became much more of a target for bullies—boys and girls.

Marylou was one of these girls. I usually managed to stay out of the path of Marylou and her friends Christina and Caesar. But one day the teacher told me to sit at their table. Reluctantly I sat in the empty seat and pretended not to notice the glares from Marylou and her friends.

"Move it!" Caesar hissed in my ear when the teacher was out of earshot. "This is our spot."

I tried to ignore them, but Marylou joined him.

"You hear me, *gringa?* I said this is our spot."

I sighed and started to get up, but the teacher saw me moving my stuff and told me to sit down again. I was relieved that they seemed to drop the issue as the teacher watched. Later, however, Christina took a piece of paper and crumpled it.

"This is you," she said, menacingly. "Nobody takes my friend's seat."

Strangely enough, although I had dreaded this and tried to avoid it all year, I felt calm. Without even thinking I looked her straight in the eye and said, "I am not afraid of you. I have someone bigger on my side."

She laughed. "Who, God?"

"Yes, that's right."

**"Well, you and your God can meet us after school. We're going to let you have it."**

"Well, you and your God can meet us after school. We're going to let you have it and then we'll see who's bigger."

Growing up I heard stories about David and Goliath, but now the reality of my claim gripped me. What if God didn't come through?

The bell rang and I slowly walked to the field outside the school. Christina and Marylou were laughing and showing their fists. I looked at them and said nothing. My silence seemed to unnerve them.

Finally, when they realized I was not going to answer them, Marylou gestured to a big girl they had chosen to beat me. "Come on, let's go. She's not worth our time," Marylou said.

The girl slapped me as they walked away, laughing loudly.

As I looked back on that incident I realized it was a sign of God's favor in my life. Shortly after that ordeal with Marylou, I was moved to a private school and didn't have to attend the even more violent middle school. When I went to high school, the other girls who bullied me all dropped out of school one by one—except Marylou.

God was faithful. He reminded me that no matter what the circumstances, if I put my trust in him, he will lift me up.

*Colleen J. Yang*

# WHEN GOD
## breaks through

Giants make us feel small. But as Colleen realized, God can dwarf any giant. David, the Old Testament king and psalm writer who took on a giant or two in his day, shouted out to God, "I know you are pleased with me, for you have not let my enemy triumph over me" (Psalm 41:11, NLT).

The "giants" of life are not always physical bullies. Fear is another intimidator that dogs our steps and nibbles at our confidence. When we face a giant we hope for a happy ending to our story. But sometimes years pass before we see the end, as Colleen experienced. Maybe that's your experience now. If so consider another psalm written by David: "You, O LORD, are a shield around me; you are my glory, the one who holds my head high" (Psalm 3:3, NLT). He gives you the courage and strength to face any giant.

## my
## CHALLENGE

What giants are you facing? What do you believe about God? Have you asked him for help? Be honest with him as you talk to him about your concerns.

# AHEAD OF THE GAME 45

## developing a **LEADER'S** voice

"You want me to play football?"

I questioned my father's faith in me—and his sanity—as we walked down the football aisle in the Dick's Sporting Goods store with my uncle slightly behind us.

"You choose if you want to do it. I'm just saying that playing football would be a really good experience for you," my dad said.

Our high school had just started a football team, and my dad and uncle both wanted me to try out. They had been outstanding football players in high school and college and even if they didn't say so directly, I knew they wanted me to carry on the family tradition.

"I don't know a thing about football," I stuttered.

My uncle's baritone voice shook my eardrums. "You can do it for one year, just to say you did it. Besides, if you are king of the field, you will be king of the school."

As they explored the merits of the different helmets, I wandered toward the window and stared into the dark evening. I didn't know if I could be a football player like the two of them were when they were my age. I'd started hearing about their football experiences earlier than I could remember. My father had played linebacker for the University of Hawaii Rainbow Warriors. My uncle had been wide receiver for the University of Iowa Hawkeyes. They told me about all the cuts and fractures they suffered. And from the time I was a baby, they told me I had the genes to play the game. I shuddered when I thought about how much pain I'd have to endure to become just half as good as they'd been. Even though I was scared, I also found some courage deep inside. From that night on, I was determined to hold up the family tradition.

Early one Monday morning I walked into the coach's room with my dad to get fitted for shoulder pads and a helmet. The maroon helmets glistened in the fluorescent light. With an eager smile my dad grabbed a large one and plopped it on my head.

As Coach Wilson pumped the helmet full of air, I felt different inside and I could see my dad's faith in me grow. My dad had so much confidence that I was going to make the team and be a great player.

After getting fitted I dashed to the field to begin my first training camp. During those two weeks I ran and fought harder than I ever had in my life. My body was wrecked at the end of camp. Maroon jersey marks lined my skin and bruises covered my body.

When we started two practices a day, I knew I was facing a long road. Conditioning was so grueling that some players threw up. I wondered why I was there.

I was completely baffled when they put me on the defensive line. I wasn't one of the bigger players on this football team. My dad had played the line, but he told me that was for really big guys and that I should be a wideout (wide receiver) near the sidelines. I was fast and had good hands when the ball came my way.

I wanted more than that. I wanted to fight to make my plays, not just run around and wait for them to come to me. I knew I was in the right place after my first hit on the front line. I loved getting past a player and sacking the quarterback.

One Saturday morning about four games into the season we were practicing for Monday's big game and, as usual, lined up for the coach's instructions.

"OK, the captains for the game on Monday are Vick and Chones."

*Wait a second! Did he just say my name? Why did he pick me? I am just a lineman. I can't lead this team onto the field.*

I stood at the back of the line looking at my teammates. The sunlight reflected off of our helmets and the smell of sweaty practice jerseys filled the air. I noticed how one other player's jersey was ripped and the pads were sticking out—the battle scars of a quarterback's jersey.

"Hey, captains! Are you going to get in the front of the line or what?"

I obeyed without any more hesitation. I had never been a leader before, much less the captain of a football team. I jogged to the front and waited for the whistle to screech.

As the whistle blew I jogged to the 45-yard line with the other captain. Chones was a wide receiver and the fastest man on our team. He stood there waiting for me to do something, looking scared just like me. We were supposed to lead our teammates in warm-ups so all eyes were on us, waiting.

"What do you do in a time like this?" I muttered under my mouth guard. "This is my chance; I have to show them what a true leader looks and sounds like. Lord, give me strength to lead these guys on the field."

*Wait a second! Did he just say my name? Why did he pick me?*

Suddenly I began shouting commands with a voice I had never heard before. It rattled my face mask. I sounded completely different, which gave me confidence. Imagine that. I gained confidence from my own voice.

"Down! Up! Down! Up! Switch!" The echoes carried past the trees at the end of the field and across the gravel of the road.

The coach heard me as he walked down to the football field. Later he told me I did a great job leading the team in warm-ups. From that moment I knew God called me to be a leader. He had given me a voice and I needed to use it to guide my team.

*Tom Vick*

# WHEN GOD
## breaks through

As he thought about taking over the leadership reigns from Moses, Joshua undoubtedly felt fear. Wouldn't you if you had to lead a nation of people into a series of battles to take the promised land? But God gave him a pep talk that would rival any coach's. "Have I not commanded you? Be strong and courageous. Do not be terrified; do not be discouraged, for the Lord your God will be with you wherever you go" (Joshua 1:9, NIV). Like Joshua, Tom discovered the power of God's presence. It was his secret weapon against fear. Is that your secret weapon as well?

## my
## CHALLENGE

What leadership roles are you contemplating? How does the message of Joshua 1:9 help as you consider your role?

## trusting in God's **SAFEGUARDS**

A year had passed since my family moved to town just before my junior year. I still felt like the new kid on the block. I just couldn't seem to fit in. Del was my salvation.

Old friends had promised to keep in touch, but we eventually stopped communicating. Students at my new school didn't seem to have room for new friendships—especially since many of them had known each other since elementary school. I felt lonely and left out.

What were my options? I could quit trying. Who would even notice? Who would care? Then Del caught my attention—and we started dating.

I worked as a snack bar waitress at a department store to earn money for my class ring. Del worked in the same store, earning money for college. He was both shy and serious. I looked for ways to make him laugh and to lighten up his more serious side. With a quick embrace or a kiss I could make him blush until his face turned almost as red as his hair! Our relationship was comfortable. I felt safe with Del as our friendship grew.

All went smoothly for a while. But eventually we felt a stronger pull toward sexual activity. We never spoke about remaining abstinent, but neither of us wanted to be swept away by the tide. We both knew others whose bad decisions had led to shame, regret, and postponed dreams.

But I was so lonely, and I wanted to feel a sense of belonging so badly. I felt so safe and sheltered in my relationship with Del. What a dangerous combination of feelings! Our beliefs that most often clearly defined what was wrong and unwise could be so conveniently ignored under other circumstances. The temptations came. Would we go down that path?

No, we wouldn't, we told each other, but we weren't exceptional. It wasn't just a matter of willpower. We resisted sexual activity because our parents and church had laid a strong spiritual foundation for us. And because Del was influenced by the protective care that he saw his father give to his sisters, and he wanted to extend that care to me. And because the guiding, loving hand of our heavenly Father did not want us to be harmed. All of those things worked in harmony to keep us abstinent.

Activity helped too.

"Got your racket? Let's go to the park and see if we can get a court."

"Grab your bike. Let's go riding. I'll meet you by the bridge at one."

Del invited me to bike around town, to play tennis—although neither of us was very good at it—to get "rich" by buying and selling Monopoly properties on summer afternoons.

**The temptations came. Would we go down that path?**

I found that the best way to build our friendship and overcome my loneliness was to be active and have fun.

We began to see more options for how to spend time together, instead of focusing on the thrills involved in touching hands or placing an arm around the shoulder. Through shared experiences, I discovered Del's humor and grew to appreciate his practical side. For example there was the matter of the birthday present.

"What did Del give you for your birthday?" my friend Sherri asked while we ate cake and ice cream. He'd given me a sweatshirt from his college in tie-dyed blue—a great color I thought. I pulled the gift from its box to show her.

"Not very romantic," she said.

I agreed. But the gift didn't need to be romantic. The friendship was its own romance and that was enough.

I respected Del for the integrity and care he showed me and for his commitment to following Jesus and doing the right thing.

More often than not, God works in our lives to guide and protect us in ways that we don't even notice. He might nudge us to choose one path over another, or give us courage to take the unpopular stand, or help us to love and care for others in ways that honor him. God is with us and we can trust him to help us.

As a result of our decision to remain pure, Del and I have remained close friends. Our relationship helped us each establish a standard for what a good relationship could be. I am thankful for decisions that resulted in no regrets and no shame.

*Karen Young*

# WHEN GOD
## breaks through

When you look at entertainment magazines or read about celebrities on the Internet, you don't hear much about abstinence. In fact the idea is often viewed as archaic, impossible, or even weird. Yet abstinence is a safeguard that protects us emotionally and physically. And it *is* possible. After all, Jesus practiced abstinence.

*Yeah, right! It was easy for him,* you might be thinking. *He didn't go through what I'm going through.* But the writer of Hebrews reminds us, "Jesus understands every weakness of ours, because he was tempted in every way that we are. But he did not sin!" (Hebrews 4:15, CEV). Note the words *he was tempted in every way that we are. But he did not sin.*

## my
## CHALLENGE

What tempts you the most? In moments of temptation do you really believe God "has your back"?

# ARE YOU QUALIFIED? 47

## trusting the Spirit's **GUIDANCE** when telling others about God

*Do I have what it takes to do this?*

That's what I wondered as I faced the group of kids. The group of wild kids. Our youth group had been leading vacation Bible school at a mission for three days while out of town on a mission trip. This had been the worst day yet. Sylvia, the ringleader and a complainer, was at her finest. Poor Renee barely got through the story she was trying to tell them. We had come to help the kids, but the Bible lessons we'd shared so far didn't seem to have gotten through to them.

*Tomorrow I have to present the plan of salvation,* I realized. All the leaders have told me, "Do your best and trust God." But I know that if I don't give them the information properly, they may not believe. Or they might believe in the wrong thing and years later doubt their salvation like I once did.

I went to the basketball court and started to shoot some baskets. While we were on the mission trip, we were staying in a host church's recreation facilities during the evening and going to the mission each day.

After I played basketball with some others for a while, I was tired but more settled. I picked up my missions trip journal and found a quiet place. I reread my entry from a couple of days before: *I'm scared I'll mess up my story. Hopefully I won't. I'm afraid some won't come back and we can't reach them. Because with a little patience and understanding and hanging around with them, we can get to these kids' hard hearts.*

I then read the next day's *Answers to Prayer* entry: *I did pretty well teaching tonight, but I now know how our Sunday school teachers feel when we don't respond right away. It's very lonely when your students do that. I hope they got the message of my story. They got the facts pretty well, but I don't know about the message. I may never know. But if one of them got it, it was worth the effort. In a couple of days I have to tell them about salvation.*

I wrote in the day's entry: *Well I really don't know if I can do it, but all I can do is my best. God will make it work. Trust and obey.*

I closed my journal, went upstairs, and stepped through the array of sleeping bags in the boys' area. I wanted to work more on my lesson, but had no more time. When the lights went off, my fears filled my mind.

As I tossed and turned, trying to think up a new way to tell an old story, I prayed silently for help to do my best and to trust God with the results.

In the morning I dragged myself from my sleeping bag. Breakfast was good, and I felt better after eating. When we arrived at the mission, the kids were as noisy as normal and I felt nervous.

## God, please help me say what you want me to say.

The craft went well. They didn't get much glue or markers on each other. Then it was time for my story and we settled them the best we could. Sylvia mouthed off that she didn't want to listen to yet another story—she wanted to make another bookmark like we did the day before. Several kids agreed and I realized I'd lost them before I started.

*God, please help me say what you want me to say.*

I began my story: "Today we're going to talk about . . ."

And a little later I ended my story: "And that's what it means to become a Christian."

Whoa! All of the kids were deathly quiet and staring straight at me. Even my teammates and the adults were frozen in place. What did I say? I couldn't remember. Did I do it right? Did I mess it up? I didn't know. Then the next person took over, and the kids revved up to full volume. I still feel like my knees wobbled as I suddenly realized that God spoke to these kids through me. He honored my request and they now had what they needed to come to him.

The next day in my journal under *Answers To Prayer* I wrote: *Two people, Sylvia and Julie, came to know Christ in our group.*

*David W. Barnett*

## WHEN GOD
### breaks through

Ever feel tongue-tied at the thought of telling someone about Christ? We think we have to persuade others with a perfect argument. If we don't, we feel we're personally responsible for turning people away from God.

Just before he was killed, Jesus told his followers about the coming of the Holy Spirit. "When the Father sends the Advocate as my representative—that is, the Holy Spirit—he will teach you everything and will remind you of everything I have told you" (John 14:26, NLT). The burden is on the Holy Spirit to convince; he just wants us to be willing to be used.

### my
## CHALLENGE

Consider the people you know who don't know God. What would you tell someone about God if you had the opportunity?

# A WHOLE NEW DREAM 48

## giving up our **PLANS** in favor of God's plans

When I was four years old, I wanted to be an oceanographer. Either that or a marine biologist. I wasn't too picky as a preschooler.

By the time I entered first grade, I could name more than 20 species of sharks (lemon, leopard, whitetip, reef, nurse, grey, white, blue, bull, wobbegong, thrasher, Port Jackson, whale, basking, Greenland, blacktip, hammerhead, tiger, mako, dogfish).

I can still do it. I *really* wanted to be a marine biologist. I was committed to studying the waters of the world. I read everything I could get my hands on. I snorkeled for hours along the south shore of Lake Ontario, where I grew up.

In our farm ponds I found bass and bluegill. In the rivers I would watch the trout run and smallmouth bass dart from the cover of the bank. I loved to be on the water, canoeing, sailing, and swimming.

This obsession did not wane as I grew. In fact it deepened. In high school I aced biology. I read and reread every book on the subject.

I took the college board achievement test in biology and aced that after long study sessions on the lakeshore. I signed up for an independent study in marine biology, besides taking chemistry and physics. I was about to realize my goal. I received a letter from the dean of the biology department from my first choice of colleges—Boston University. Not only did it have the nation's top-ranked marine biology department at the time, it was in Boston, my favorite city.

In my junior year I began the admissions process. I gathered the necessary material and started filling out forms and writing essays. Not too difficult for me, having thought about this for the past 13 years. Boston, here I come.

So how did I end up applying to a small Bible college I'd never visited (or heard of) in a city I had never been to, to study international ministry? The short answer is that God told me to. The long answer? A little more involved.

Early in my junior year I got a small, creeping feeling that God was going to change the direction of my life. I felt, for some strange reason, that he wanted me to be a missionary. Like any good Christian who first trusted Christ at age five, I resisted. I could feel the Spirit's prompting and tried to fight it. I said I would do that later, after a successful career as a world-renown expert on shark behavior. Just let me go to Boston; let me study for a while. I could get a full ride, which would be a huge benefit to my family.

I argued with God—how could he expect me to change *now?* Why did he let me go through my whole life with a dream, only to dash it within months of its beginning? All those hours studying, swimming, and reading felt like a waste of time. Plus I would have to tell everyone that, despite all the years of saying I would be a marine biologist, I was actually going to be a missionary. I did not like to change my mind, especially without a good reason.

Why was I going into ministry? Because God told me to. To a scientific mind, that did not seem to work. Everything in my life seemed to lead

**I argued with God— how could he expect me to change *now?***

to my inevitable publication in *National Geographic* with a yearly feature on Discovery Channel's Shark Week.

Plus I was not missionary material. I did not particularly enjoy telling others about Christ. I wanted a sports car and a sailboat. I wanted to work on a tricked-out research vessel, anchored off the Great Barrier Reef in Australia. I did not want to end up in some small European town, struggling to learn the language. Nor did I want to contract a rare and deadly tropical disease while trekking through the Amazon basin (though I would have enjoyed the wildlife). I was a little upset.

So in November of my junior year with applications half-filled out, I was still hoping the dream could continue. And then God pulled out the big guns, along with a little, rather unfair, coercion. It was time for the annual missions festival at my home church. I thought, *OK, I can hold out, I can make it through this.*

The first weekend was fine. A couple of very nice people told amazing stories of how God was working in Central America. *Great, I appreciate their hard work.* However, during the closing weekend, the speakers were a husband and wife team working as missionaries in France. *OK, I like France, no problem.* Then the husband told what they did in France: they ran a ski camp in the Alps.

Next to being on the water, my favorite activity was skiing. Loved it, couldn't get enough.

Once I let my plan go, once I told God "OK, you win," it was incredible. I felt as if I had been freed. All the wrestling and doubt, the struggle to keep the dream alive, melted away. I was ready to do whatever God asked of me and found great joy in that—greater joy than I ever experienced studying or snorkeling or sailing. It was indescribable.

I talked with one of the missionaries from France after the service. He told me he studied at Moody Bible Institute, which was one of the top missions schools in the country. I had never heard of it. Our pastor had a five-year-old catalog from the school. I took it, sent in the application, and a year and a half later, watched as my family pulled out of the parking lot for the 11-hour drive back to New York. I was in Chicago, ready to start a whole new dream.

*Mark R. Nesbitt*

## WHEN GOD
### breaks through

Like Mark, you've probably made plans for your life. Who hasn't? Perhaps like Mark you can relate to this truth written in the book of Proverbs: "You can make many plans, but the Lord's purpose will prevail" (Proverbs 19:21, NLT). Sounds scary and frustrating, doesn't it? Sometimes our plans coincide with God's, other times they diverge. Many people fear asking God what he wants for their lives because they think he'll ask them to do something they don't want to do.

But check it out: The Lord says, "I will guide you along the best pathway for your life. I will advise you and watch over you" (Psalm 32:8, NLT). *The best pathway*—not the worst or most repellent. The best. Only the best for a beloved child, right?

### my
## CHALLENGE

Are you willing to take your plans and tell God, "I'm ready to do whatever you ask of me" as Mark did? If not, what's stopping you? Be honest with God.

## allowing the **FEAR** of God to mold character

When I was 13, a teacher pulled me aside in the hallway. "I saw you talking and laughing during the assembly," she said. "Our speaker could hardly talk over all that noise. I thought you knew how to behave better than that."

Then she said the words that made me feel sick: "I'm going to the office to call your mother."

For the rest of the day I felt tangible fear. Mom wouldn't hit me. She wouldn't even yell at me. But her eyes would be big and sad. She would say, "I thought I taught you better than that."

I knew full well how wrong it was to let her down. I imagined that God would react something like my mom. He'd be sad. Maybe he'd heave a big sigh.

I could justify what I'd done of course. My friends were talking. I simply joined in. It shouldn't be such a big deal. It was only talking. But I knew the speaker was saying things I needed to hear. I could imagine what it must feel like to be a teacher and have your students ignore you.

I was brought up to be respectful. I really had no excuse for violating my inner sense of right and wrong. If only the teacher hadn't seen me talking, my mom wouldn't know. God would know—but in the larger scheme of things it was such a tiny event.

*If only, if only,* I thought. *What good are the "if onlys"? A wrong thing is still a wrong thing even if no one sees it.*

So I spent the day preparing my speech for Mom. I would tell her I was sorry. I might even say I'd write the speaker an apology.

That afternoon I braced myself as I walked in the door of our house. I felt cold. Mom came out from the kitchen. Her eyes weren't big and sad. She smiled and asked how my day was. Then I knew the teacher never called my house. I'd spent the day worrying for nothing.

I went to my room and prayed, asking God to forgive me. Suddenly I realized the teacher who'd pulled me aside in the hallway had acted as God's messenger. She brought my conscience to life again after it had been sleeping for a while.

**I'd spent the day worrying for nothing.**

I went back to the living room. "Mom," I began, "I'd better tell you about my day. . . ."

The only way I could breathe easily again was to confess everything. My mom said, "You know you did wrong and I can see that you're sorry. I think you learned a lot today. Now give me a hug!"

And I could feel God hugging me too!

*Judith Costello*

## WHEN GOD
### breaks through

When you were a kid, maybe the fear of what a parent or some other authority figure might do kept you out of trouble. But Judith also discovered the value of another source of fear. The writer of Proverbs 16 sums it up succinctly: "By fearing the LORD, people avoid evil" (Proverbs 16:6, NLT). Knowing that God sees all and grieves when we mess up can put on the brakes when it comes to wrong behaviors.

### my
## CHALLENGE

What do you fear? Are you more afraid of looking bad in front of your friends or in front of God? Consider what you value most: your reputation or God's.

# THE GRIZZLY AND THE AIR-CONDITIONER 50

## experiencing the **GRACE** of God

I grew up with a grizzly bear. Sort of. It was a rug. My dad shot him up in Montana or someplace in the early '60s. He was made into a rug, with glassy eyes and an open roaring mouth.

Maybe it's because of that rug we also called my dad the grizzly.

Of course I called him that respectfully. In North Mississippi we follow two rules: one, never talk back to your parents and two, don't even think about buying anything of value without an air-conditioner included. House, car, office space, whatever. The humidity in this part of the world is horrible. We don't have any wind to help relieve this smothering blanket. No one jogs. No one does *anything* fast. When you grow up here, you understand why the Mississippi Delta is the true "home of the blues." You can't sing those songs right unless you have experienced Mississippi in July and August.

So we had an air-conditioner—a very nice outside unit. But when it stopped cooling well, my mother called a repairman and he examined it carefully.

"You're getting clogged up here in the back—see all those leaves and seeds from that mimosa tree? You need to hose off your outside unit once in a while to keep the air flow going." He used our water hose to clear off the vents, freeing it of debris.

My mother didn't have one ounce of mechanical skill. She had me stand beside her and watch as the repairman hosed our unit, and asked, "Honey, do you see what he's doing? Can you do that?" I assured her I could. He took his check and went his merry way.

Over the next few weeks I took care of my family's comfort. I hosed the air-conditioner every chance I got. I even took off the back and hosed the inside of the unit, where the motor was. The unit stopped working. My mother asked if I was hosing it.

"Yes, ma'am!" I said.

The serviceman came again and asked the same question. Proudly I told him how I not only hosed the outside, but the inside as well.

"Ma'am, you are going to need a new unit," he told my mother.

I was devastated. It was 94 degrees out with a heat index of over 102. We were melting. I had killed our friend. My mother went inside to discuss the terms with the serviceman for a new unit.

I stood in our backyard, trying to wish the unit back to life. I shook it. I kicked it. I spun the dead blades with my hands, hoping to resuscitate it.

Then my dad came home. A Ford F100 pickup has a distinct sound. The driver's side door opened and closed. At 6' 3", 230 pounds, this former Marine and now a truck driver for Missouri Pacific Truck Lines could not enter any home, building, office or dock without people being aware of his presence. He entered our home and talked to my mother, then came out the back door.

He stood in a work shirt bearing his company's logo. He was sweaty and grimy and his blue jeans drooped from working all day in the merciless heat. He looked at me with a stunned expression.

"Dad, I blew up the air-conditioner," I confessed.

**We were melting. I had killed our friend.**

He hung his head and then did something truly amazing: he laughed. He laughed and laughed and shook his head and laughed some more, a low laugh that grew in warmth and belied all ill will.

It was my turn to be stunned. "You're not angry?"

He shook his head and explained. "Son, this morning I got a speeding ticket on the way to work. At work my boss chewed me out and gave me a warning letter. If I get one more in the next six months, I'm fired. On the way home I got a flat tire on my truck, which took an hour to fix."

He smiled a Kentucky boy's smile at me and said, "Son, sometimes you just gotta laugh or you'll go crazy."

I couldn't believe it. He wasn't going to yell at me? I tried again. "I'm really sorry, Dad."

"Don't worry about it. We'll figure it out. Come on inside for supper."

I obeyed.

I don't remember a lot of things my dad said growing up, but that day always sticks in my mind. That blistering hot day, my dad showed me what grace really is. I did what I thought was right and ruined things for everyone. I expected wrath and judgment from the grizzly and I knew I deserved it.

But the grizzly didn't bite. He just laughed. At that moment my father showed me that he loved me more than I knew. He loved me more than his own comfort and he loved me for being honest.

*Justice Carmon*

## WHEN GOD
### breaks through

Have you ever thought about what grace is? It is withholding punishment to provide "undeserved kindness" (Romans 3:23, NLT). The apostle Paul explained it this way:

> *The sin of this one man, Adam, brought death to many. But even greater is God's wonderful grace and his gift of forgiveness to many through this other man, Jesus Christ. And the result of God's gracious gift is very different from the result of that one man's sin. For Adam's sin led to condemnation, but God's free gift leads to our being made right with God, even though we are guilty of many sins (Romans 5:15–16, NLT).*

Grace is yours for the asking. But first you have to know you need it.

### my
## CHALLENGE

When have you experienced undeserved kindness? How did that make you feel? Does someone in your life need undeserved kindness or your forgiveness? How will you offer it?

# A MUSICAL MOMENT 51

## reaching **OUT** through music

I sang in the madrigal choir during high school. The madrigal choir focused on tone quality and pure vocal performance. Many of the arrangements were technically complex, offering vocal challenges. The group performed only a cappella, so we had no instrumental backup to cover our mistakes. We often performed in distinctive renaissance attire, providing a visual backdrop to the music.

One Sunday in early December the madrigal choir performed at my church. This performance took place near the beginning of the two morning worship services. That setting and the timeless beauty of the music gave me a sense of the original intent of the composers and the message they were trying to convey in music.

Since we attended the first service, most of us slipped out of the sanctuary after our second performance. Three of us decided it was time for brunch, even though we were still wearing our Elizabethan attire. We certainly got some surprised looks as we entered a local restaurant!

The waitress commented that it was nice to have a visit from members of a madrigal choir. When she finished writing down our orders, she paused. Then she leaned over the table and whispered, "My mother is here today celebrating her eightieth birthday. Would you sing for her?"

The waitress asked us if we knew the song "Lo, How a Rose E'er Blooming." We looked at each other, smiling. It was one of our favorites and we had performed it twice that morning. We were sure it would work, though we were missing a part. I was the tenor, my friend the baritone, and the young lady with us was a soprano.

The waitress added, "I want to ask one more favor. I sang in high school and know the alto part. May I sing with you?"

We walked over to a table where a silver-haired lady sat alone having breakfast. She noticed her daughter approaching and then looked questioningly at us. We formed a semicircle, hummed a soft pitch note, and began to sing. The chaos in the restaurant quieted by the time we reached the end of the first line. The stillness seemed as holy to me as what I felt in church that morning. When we finished there wasn't a sound. Everyone heard our waitress say, "Happy Birthday, Mom."

We walked back to our table amid appreciative nods and quiet words of thanks. I had already felt great about the opportunity to sing for those in my church. Little did I know we'd have another chance to touch others' lives. Perhaps the people in that restaurant needed to hear the words of our song even more than those who had gathered for worship that morning. The waitress's mother came by our table later to thank us for making her birthday special and bringing Christmas to the restaurant.

**The stillness seemed as holy to me as what I felt in church that morning.**

Now that I am in college, I miss music as a scheduled part of my school days. I miss the friendships and the harmony. I miss the power of the music to move me and inspire the audience. But when I look back on that Christmas moment in the restaurant, I realize music was the language we were using to communicate. Our message created a connection between us and the people who listened. It renewed a bond between a daughter and her mother. And it celebrated the link God wants to have with us.

The last verse of the carol we sang speaks directly to the Christ child. I felt that by singing to Jesus in that restaurant we believed he was actually there to listen. Somehow remembering Jesus in that place has made me much more aware of him in my life. I've finally realized what "practicing the presence of

Christ" means. It means more than believing Christ is everywhere. I practice the presence of Christ when I expect to meet him and communicate with him everywhere I go—even in restaurants.

*Spencer N. as told to Neil Wilson*

# WHEN GOD
## breaks through

Telling someone about God isn't always about having the right words. Sometimes having the right tune helps. God can use anything to get his message out. That's why the apostle Paul could proclaim, "Let the message about Christ completely fill your lives, while you use all your wisdom to teach and instruct each other. With thankful hearts, sing psalms, hymns, and spiritual songs to God" (Colossians 3:16, CEV).

## my
## CHALLENGE

In what ways can you "practice the presence of Christ"?

# THE "BORING" LIFE 52

## discovering the **POWER** of living for Christ

High school was fairly easy for me. No big problems, no issues to speak of. That embarrassed me a bit when I went to college. In the Christian college I attended, my friends talked about their lives in high school before they'd found Christ. They laughed about the parties, the drinking, the drugs, and all the crazy—even hilarious—things they had done.

*Hmmm, I trusted Christ at age five,* I'd think. *What did I do before that? Picked on my little brother, fought with my older sister. . . . And let's not forget the time Mom told me to pick up my toys and I refused.*

I felt I had no stories and nothing that pointed to the incredible transforming power of God's Spirit. My friends told how God pulled them out of drug addiction, destructive lifestyles, and terrible circumstances. I grew up in a loving, supportive Christian family. Even my extended family was mostly Christian. I had cousins who were pastors, sisters who were missionaries, and parents who taught Sunday school and Awana.

Kids in my public school pretty much accepted me for who I was. My school was too small to have many cliques, and most of us crossed clique lines anyway. We had "schlocks"—National Honor Society members who excelled in athletics; "freageeks"—hip, cool artists who were in the Math, Science and Computer Clubs; and even "gearbanders"—motorheads who played first-chair trumpet in the band. So we all pretty much got along. My faith wasn't an issue. I could follow Christ and still hang out with everyone.

Early in my freshman year, however, I attended a sleepover at a friend's house and someone pulled out dirty movies, stolen beer, and other forms of high school malfeasance. Instead of partying I read *Sports Illustrated* for most of the night.

Before this not much distinguished me from those who didn't follow Christ. But by not participating in the "rites of passage," I chose my side. I figured I'd lose friends, but what could I do? I wanted to please Christ. My faith was real to me.

The evening passed uneventfully. Even though my friends didn't say too much that night, I figured my life as part of "normal" high school society was over. I spent the weekend preparing for the coming onslaught of mockery.

On Monday a guy I didn't know very well but who'd been at the party, came to me and said he wanted to shake the hand of a moral man. I thought, *Ha, ha! Is that the best you can come up with?*

**I chose my side. I figured I'd lose friends, but what could I do?**

I shook his hand and walked away. But several times that day, he came back to me and said the same thing.

I wanted to say, "This isn't working! I don't feel shame or regret. In fact I am taking it as a compliment."

Then I realized it was a compliment. He was serious.

God had taken care of me. I expected to live my high school existence as an outcast, but instead I found a friend. We remained best friends throughout high school. I was the best man at his wedding. Even the other guys at the party stayed my good friends. It became an unspoken agreement that if the party focused on one or more elements I would not engage in, I was out; if it was just a bunch of friends hanging out, I was in. A détente was reached.

*Mark R. Nesbitt*

# WHEN GOD
## breaks through

Perhaps you wonder if the story of how you became a believer would convince anyone to become a Christian, especially if it doesn't seem dramatic. But *anyone* who believes in Jesus has been transformed. The apostle Paul put it this way: "I have been crucified with Christ and I no longer live, but Christ lives in me. The life I live in the body, I live by faith in the Son of God, who loved me and gave himself for me" (Galatians 2:20, NIV). Maybe you didn't have to face a near drug overdose or an arrest to get you to God. But the fact that you have a relationship with him is still a miracle.

## my
## CHALLENGE

Have you told anyone the story of how you became a believer? Your story can be an encouragement to someone. What would you tell someone about your faith in God? Make it a point to tell someone about your faith journey this week.

# LOST IN GOD 53

## finding **FRIENDSHIP** and hope through God's love

Even though Geoffrey and I lived on two different continents separated by an enormous ocean, we shared something that filled both of our souls: loneliness.

I sat at Starbucks that night, sipping my coffee as I read Geoffrey's letter. His expression of distress caught me off guard and my heart went out to him.

Geoffrey Kawoya lives in Uganda with his grandmother and takes good care of his family. I know him because he is my Compassion child. My family sends money through Compassion International to support him. We also send letters to him. Initially Geoffrey communicated with us by letting a translator write his letters, until he learned how to write in English. Now he writes us twice a month with a hope that sometimes I cannot quite understand.

Geoffrey is 17, like me, and goes to school. He is a Christian in a mostly Muslim community, and recently Muslims have killed Christians in Uganda. Sometimes I wish we could hire a guard to protect Geoffrey.

When we first adopted Geoffrey as our Compassion child, he was eight or nine. He was a Christian long before I ever met him through the letters, but he didn't know a lot about God. His prayer life was simple, as he prayed to God for his family and their health.

Through years of reading his letters, I watched his faith grow. He loved hearing about God in church. He also got more excited about school—

especially enjoying math and participating in track and field. Geoffrey also shared a few songs with us in one letter and always thanked us for sponsoring him. Lately he had been expressing his faith to us. We gave him a Bible in his language so he could study more. This led him to write the most recent and astonishing letter.

I picked up the letter again and read more.

*This month I've been really talking to God. Not out loud, just in my head. He's always there. And I got to thinking, "Why?" Why is he always spending time with me? So I started to read the Bible and an idea came to me. God loves us because he made us. And he made us because he wanted to be with us. I think about it. Of all things he could have done, he wanted to make us.*

**That is the end of my SELF-ESTeem.**

At the end of his letter, Geoffrey wrote something profound: *That is the end of my SELF-ESTeem.* This sentence, broken English and all, is packed with meaning. Geoffrey, in a very simple way, said he had come to the end of himself and was letting God take control of his life. He was losing himself in God.

Sitting in Starbucks, thousands of miles from Geoffrey, I thought about what he said about giving himself totally to the Lord. Then I thought about my friends, a group of guys who loved to "airsoft"—a popular hobby at my school involving shooting targets with BB guns. We had formed an airsoft team. I had tried to share my faith with them, but they just brushed it aside. They were afraid of God and what he might do in their lives. Still I loved them like my brothers, and even though we had different beliefs, they accepted me.

Then I realized that I was becoming like them. I started to forget about God and what he thought about me.

When that happened I thought of Geoffrey and how close he'd been growing to God. If he went to my school, would he want me to be friends with these people?

I had to admit it would be difficult to break away from this group of friends. We had been through so much together. But I felt like God was pulling me away from them. Who would I hang out with?

Again Geoffrey came to mind. He had given up himself to follow God and his will. Geoffrey didn't care what people thought about him. He just listened to God. I realized God loves Geoffrey and me the same way. And now God was telling me to throw away my bad friendships and follow him. So I made the toughest decision I had ever made—I quit the airsoft team.

Now, like Geoffrey, I am alone. Even though Geoffrey and I feel lonely now, God has given us hope from his great love for us. And God has provided Geoffrey and me with a special bond that reaches across continents, oceans, and cultures to encourage and support each other.

*Tom Vick*

## WHEN GOD
### breaks through

Who hasn't felt lonely at times? While on the one hand, Tom can echo with the psalmist, "I lie awake, lonely as a solitary bird on the roof" (Psalm 102:7, NLT). Like David he can also admit, "I am a friend to anyone who fears you—anyone who obeys your commandments" (Psalm 119:63, NLT). Tom's friendship with Geoffrey challenged him to accept the possibility of loneliness as he strove to obey God.

## my
## CHALLENGE

Make a list of your friends. In what ways do your friends challenge you? Are there some friendships you feel the nudge to let go of as Tom did?

# BURNT SHOES 54

## discovering God's IMPRINT

Playing capture the flag in the dark with flashlights was not for me. The other teens on this youth group campout could do that. I enjoyed my youth group and the people in it, but I was a senior and I'd had my share of the pranks and random silliness that somehow overtake a group of teens after too many marshmallows roasted over an open fire. No, sitting by the fire was probably a much better, saner, and safer option for me.

So I sat by the campfire, enjoying its calm crackle, punctuated by remote screams, cheers, and grunts from the open meadow nearby. The evening was peaceful and I was becoming introspective. I put my feet on the ring of rocks around the fire to keep warm in the cool September night air. My thoughts turned to what it would be like to be out of high school and moving on to new challenges.

High school had been good, but like most of my peers, I felt I'd grown beyond teenage drama and sentimentality. I was ready to be an adult, with all the privileges, responsibilities, and—especially—the freedoms.

Caught up in my thoughts, I didn't notice right away that someone sat across from me. It was Eric, a new freshman in the group, a friend of a friend of a friend. We had spoken a couple of times. He hadn't been too excited about playing capture the flag, so he had watched for a little while and then returned to the campfire.

Eric shared a locker with a freshman from our church, which is how he came to our church and this campout. We talked about what it was like for him to be starting high school. Our conversation drifted all over the place but finally came to the topic of faith. Eric's family went to church on major holidays, but belief had little impact on their daily lives. I asked Eric if he thought real Christianity was different, and we got so wrapped up in our conversation that it was awhile before I noticed the smell of burning rubber.

My shoes! The campfire flame was too near my rubber soles, and they were smoking! I whirled and stamped my feet in the cold grass. The smoking stopped, but the ridges of the stones permanently indented the rubber soles of my shoes.

Eric and I laughed and kept talking. But I was amazed that my shoes told a true story: We can dance around the ring of faith as long as we want, but never be truly impacted. It takes feeling the heat, knowing the warmth and fulfillment that come only from believing, to cause permanent life change. And the fire didn't just change my shoes. Every footprint my shoes left after that fireside encounter had a distinctive mark, in the same way Jesus leaves a mark in every believer's heart that is permanent.

**We got so wrapped up in our conversation that it was awhile before I noticed the smell of burning rubber.**

Eric was ready for a life change. We talked a bit more to be sure he understood what it means to follow Christ. And then his locker partner, Bryan, returned from playing capture the flag just in time to pray with us. Eric and Bryan celebrated with loud whoops and vigorous slaps on the back and a couple of high fives.

"Awesome, dude!" they said over and over.

The campout ended as every normal campout does: During the night, the guys decided to pick up and collapse the girls' tents as the girls slept. The girls retaliated by attracting wildlife into the guys' sleeping area with food, so when guys woke up they had an interesting welcoming committee. Everyone was sore, tired, and dazed in the morning from capture the flag and coming off a sugar high. But unlike every other campout, at this one Eric had found new life and his high school years were marked with the exciting transformation that comes only from a personal relationship with Jesus Christ.

Last Sunday I saw Eric in church, his father sitting by him. Eric's new life has become contagious and his father is discovering the same truth Eric did—faith is a personal, life-changing adventure that imprints the heart with joy.

*Heather Pleier*

# WHEN GOD
## breaks through

Just as every snowflake or fingerprint is different, so is God's imprint on a life. Faith marks us as belonging to God. A well-known verse in Hebrews describes faith this way: "The fundamental fact of existence is that this trust in God, this faith, is the first foundation under everything that makes life worth living. It's our handle on what we can't see" (Hebrews 11:1, MSG). Sounds simple, doesn't it? But sometimes we complicate even the simplest acts. We think we have to create faith in the factory of our brain or heart. We pull the lever. Out pops faith. *OK, I can feel myself believing now*. But any "faith" we manufacture won't transform us. Faith in God begins when we're willing to set aside unbelief and trust God. It is an acknowledgment that we can't do it (have faith) on our own. Faith comes from God and is yours for the asking.

## my
## CHALLENGE

How has someone's faith impacted you? Have you ever told that person what his or her life means to you? Why not do so this week. What kind of impact would you like your faith to have on someone? What do you need to do or change now to make sure your life has that impact?

# SHOOTING BASKETBALLS, NOT BULLETS 55

## demolishing the **LINES** between enemies

My house in Memphis doesn't have a white picket fence. There's no swing on the front porch, no flowers by the walk. Life is grim. With no father at home, my two brothers and I hit the streets in turn to find money for food, rent, and bills.

Ours is a ride-with-me, die-with-me life, one where you learn to recognize friend from foe. As a gang member, you grant a reverse form of respect to the toughest, meanest, and deadliest of these. Without expecting to see twenty, we live hard and fast with few rules.

At fifteen, I'm already middle-aged.

Once I started to hang with the boys, I skipped school and my grades dropped. Although I liked school, I thought, *That dream's for fools. I have a quota to fill, drugs to sell, guys to shake. I've got no time for reading and studying. There are other things I gotta do.*

Ma would hassle me. "Boy, you'd better get your butt back in that classroom! Your pop's run off, your brothers are on crack, and I ain't losin' you."

"Aw, Ma! You don't know what you're talking about." Slamming the door, I headed out to blow off steam. *She just doesn't understand. I'm a man now.* I huddled deeper into my coat and turned up the next block, noting that one dilapidated house here is much like the other with iron bars on the windows and on the doors.

Seeing one of my cousins on the corner where Washington meets Parkway, I called, "Yo, James, wassup?"

"Hey, man," he said, tossing his cigarette. "I'm trying to figure out that sign." He pointed to the First Baptist Church sign up the street that read,

*All come, free basketball and hot meal Mondays 5–8.* "What do you think?"

"I hear they have a sweet indoor court. You wanna check it out tonight?"

Thinking a minute James agreed, persuaded by a potential pickup game and a hot meal. "Cool. But what if the Bloods show up?"

"Man, we'll get there first and set our ground. Meet me here 'round five."

That decision changed my life forever.

Five-fifteen was face-off time. The Crips challenged the Bloods in a man-to-man rivalry that had nothing to do with gang fighting. To our surprise, a massive black man known as Coach Mac, a youth worker who used the facilities of the mostly white church, met us when we arrived.

"You boys are welcome to play ball if you drop your colors at the door," he said. Looking us straight in the eye, he added, "Here you're not Crips or Bloods or Vice Lords. There are only three rules: no cursing, no drugs, no weapons. We're gonna shoot basketballs, not bullets."

*Fine by me,* I thought as I removed my blue hat and shirt—Crips colors—and relinquished the knife from my side pocket. I was happy to escape the reality of the streets and just be a kid for awhile.

Coach didn't seem surprised by what I handed over; he just stood there waiting. Shrugging to each other, James and I removed the extra knives we kept in our socks.

"Thanks, guys," Coach Mac said.

Eyeing those we knew to be our enemies, we kept a sharp lookout for trouble. After an hour of intense basketball, Coach called for a time-out. "Hit the bleachers!"

## "Here, you're not Crips or Bloods or Vice Lords."

Walking off the court I grumbled, "Man, I knew there'd be a catch!"

When we all sat down, Coach grabbed our attention with his low voice. "I know what it's like to walk in your shoes, to feel desperate, doomed. From this point on, you're not alone. Every week you can come play ball, eat dinner, and get help with your studies. All I ask is you give me 90 seconds to share a word with you. I promise it won't be any longer—no catch."

I looked up at his last two words. Coach's eyes burned straight through me. It was like he could see all my sins and all my dreams wrapped up together—and it was OK. When he smiled, my heart took a turn.

He opened up a raggedy leather Bible and read from Proverbs 3:1–2 (NLT), "My child, never forget the things I have taught you. Store my commands in your heart. If you do this, you will live many years, and your life will be satisfying." Coach surveyed the room and said, "You can change your ways and have a long life. I'm here to help." Bowing his head he prayed, "God, protect these boys until we meet again. Amen." He raised his head and said, "You can call me any time. Now, who's got next?"

Reaching for the ball at my feet, I glanced at my watch and realized Coach had lived up to his word—less than 90 seconds. I couldn't believe it!

Soon the same dudes we once tangled with during the week were the ones we cheered from the sidelines on Monday night. As we became more comfortable with the program, we started to bring our schoolbooks for after-dinner tutoring with volunteers from the neighborhood.

It was like Jesus himself reached to me when Coach wrapped his big hands around my heart and refused to let go. Coach's unique way of reaching out to those of us on a crooked path changed our lives. He became a friend, someone we respected and grew to love. Many of us drew away from gang activities and even started to excel in school.

Coach convinced me to try out for the Central High basketball team. He pushed me to be honorable, to do things that would make God proud. He freed me from hopelessness. His encouragement, often the only positive words I'd hear all week, stayed with me.

When I started slacking at school, he got in my face. "Tony, you can't play ball forever; you've got to stayed focused." Coach was hard, but he only wanted to make us better. He was always saying, "With freedom comes responsibility."

*With freedom comes responsibility.* I exchanged my knife for a basketball, my hate for hope. Although I haven't broken all ties with my boys, I have stopped dealing drugs and breaking the law. Coach Mac says that God loves me like a son, no matter what I've done. The way I look at it, if he is willing to love me unconditionally like that, then I had better live up to my responsibilities. That means being honorable at school, at home with Ma, and hanging out with my friends. For the most part the guys seem to respect my decisions. When

they don't, I leave, as simple as that. I'm still learning about this freedom from God. I know I have a long way to go, but I keep reaching for more—one game at a time.

*Tony P. as told to Tama Joy Westman*

## WHEN GOD
### breaks through

Coach Mac's words echoed what Jesus said: "Everyone to whom much was given, of him much will be required, and from him to whom they entrusted much, they will demand the more" (Luke 12:48, ESV). The apostle Paul undoubtedly agreed, because many years later he wrote, "You, my brothers, were called to be free. But do not use your freedom to indulge the sinful nature; rather, serve one another in love" (Galatians 5:13, NIV). So what's the point? As Tony learned, the freedom God offers encourages us to try to ace life, instead of getting by on Cs or Ds or even Fs. This includes living unselfishly, helping others, and choosing to do what pleases God.

### my
## CHALLENGE

Reread the verses above. What does freedom mean for you? What do you think is your responsibility toward the people around you? Rewrite those verses, filling in the blanks below:

You, _____, were called to be free. But do not use your freedom to _____ or _____ or _____. Rather, _____ and _____ in love.

## meeting Jesus through a **STRANGER**

"Girls, tonight is going to be the best night of camp. You are totally going to love it!"

I had been to senior high camp the previous summer, but this was the first time for my two best friends, Dana and Caroline. Tonight was Commitment Night. The auditorium would be packed. We would enjoy cool worship songs and skits, and campers would be able to make commitments to God if they wanted to. Commitment Night had really made an impact on me the year before, so I was pumped that Dana and Caroline would get to experience it.

We helped each other put the finishing touches on our outfits, makeup, and hair. Even though the focus of Commitment Night was God, we were also interested in which boys we might bump into. This camp was filled with hot guys from other schools; we figured it was our duty to be completely aware of our surroundings! Plus it was really cool to sing songs to God with a bunch of other people our age—especially if we were sitting close to those cute boys while the worship band played!

We raced to the auditorium after we finished cleanup duty in the kitchen at our group's cottage. We were so relieved that our leaders weren't making us sit as a group tonight. We were supposed to go as individuals so we could have "individual" experiences. Whatever! Everybody knew Dana, Caroline, and I were inseparable. Tonight shouldn't be any different, right?

Only a few seats were available near the back of the auditorium, when we arrived. While we waited for the program to start, we talked about our favorite parts of the day and planned how we would spend our afternoon free time the next day. That was the best time for meeting boys, and there was only one full day of camp left so we had to be smart with every moment.

As we talked we kept our eyes open for the boys we had begun to like. Dana and Caroline waved to the guys they especially liked. I wasn't so lucky though. David, that cute guy who I had spotted earlier in the evening, wasn't anywhere to be seen.

The band started playing at 7 p.m. We stood and danced and sang with all the fast songs. Then we swayed back and forth with the slow songs. I was amazed at how beautiful the songs were that night—much prettier than I remembered them being the year before. I even closed my eyes a couple of times and just listened to the words. At the end of one song, a tear dripped down my face. *What in the world?* That had never happened before. *What's going on?* I wondered.

I started to wipe the tear away but decided to leave it. Normally I would have cared about what my friends thought, but for some reason I just wanted to take in the moment.

**At the end of one song, a tear dripped down my face. *What in the world?***

As the drama team performed their skit about Jesus giving his life for us on the cross, I felt like the only one in the room. I didn't feel like talking or checking out boys or even looking at Caroline or Dana. I was completely still.

Finally the time came for making commitments. We could go to the front of the auditorium to pray if we wanted to give our lives to Jesus for the first time or recommit our lives to him. Even though I was already a Christian and had recommitted my life to him the previous summer, I immediately got out of my chair when the speaker gave the invitation. This was so unlike me. Normally I'd check to see if my friends were going forward. But not tonight. Something was really different.

Everything seemed to be in slow motion. I walked into the aisle with my head down. I didn't really know what was going on or what I would do when I got to the front, but I knew I just needed to move forward. *Left. Right. Left. Right.* I took slow, careful steps. *Left. Right.* Suddenly I noticed someone standing in front of me in the aisle. This boy's back was to the stage and he was planted right in the middle of the aisle. I started to walk around him, but he reached out to me. His arms were wide open, like he wanted to give me a hug.

Without even thinking, I let him hug me. I hugged him back, and he said, "I love you." Then he let go and smiled as he looked straight into my eyes. I continued walking toward the stage, but glanced back and saw him give a hug to every student who walked past.

When I got to the stage, I knelt and prayed. I started listening to God in a way I had never listened before. He showed me that I had been living selfishly. Everything in the room drifted away as I prayed. Nothing else deserved my attention as much as Jesus did—not the latest clothes or cute guys or what other people thought.

In the cabin that night, I was quiet and happy. Others in our group had seen the boy hugging people in the aisle. Our leaders told us about him; they didn't know his name, but they knew he was our age and had a terminal disease.

Everything started to make sense. I had met a stranger that night who knew Jesus so closely that he couldn't keep it to himself. He didn't know how many days he had left on earth, so he wanted to live each one for Jesus. I felt honored to meet him and even more honored to know Jesus, the one who had captured the guy's heart. Jesus had met me in that aisle in the embrace of a stranger. Now I had met him too, and said "yes" to his ways.

*Betsy Zenz*

# WHEN GOD
## breaks through

True discipleship is costly. Jesus made that clear to his disciples when he told them, "If anyone would come after me, he must deny himself and take up his cross and follow me" (Matthew 16:24, NIV). The disciples knew exactly what taking up the cross meant—true commitment, risking death, no turning back. This was no small decision. We may not be asked to risk our lives, but following Jesus may mean giving up certain activities, cooling off certain relationships, or changing our attitude about others. It may mean thinking about God and what he wants rather than about how we look, what we're going to wear, or how we can entertain ourselves. Betsy thought she had committed to follow Jesus, but realized other pursuits had become more important. It took a stranger's embrace to make her realize what it truly meant to live each day for Jesus.

## my
## CHALLENGE

Reflect on your commitment to God. How is your spiritual life similar to Betsy's in her story? How is it different? What steps could you take to become closer to God? Tell a trusted friend or adult what you plan to do to take that next step. Then do it!

## trusting God to **FILL** the emptiness

Maybe things would have been different if I hadn't gotten my braces off that year.

I had known Blake since seventh grade. He was a star athlete, goodlooking—he had it all. But in high school, now that I no longer had "metal mouth," he suddenly noticed me. He stared at me while the yearbook photographer took photos of the girls' sophomore basketball team. As I left the shoot, one of Blake's friends whispered to me, "He thinks you look really good."

The next Saturday night, Blake came up to me at a party and said, "You look so hot."

I laughed, playing it cool. Other guys told me I looked good too, but Blake was the best-looking, most popular guy in my class. We flirted for awhile.

On Monday he passed me a note in school. "I can't get over how hot you look. Will you go out with me?"

Soon I was no longer riding the bus home after school but would go with Blake to his house. We saw each other every day and soon became sexually active. Sometimes I told my parents I was staying overnight at a friend's house, but I'd stay at Blake's instead. He lived alone with his father, and his father let us sleep together in Blake's bedroom.

I hid the sexual activity from my parents who were Christians and had raised me to go to church. I knew about God and right and wrong, but I didn't take what I heard to heart. And now I was so busy with Blake and the popular crowd that I didn't take time to think about God. I was going to parties, getting drunk, trying drugs, having sex—just drifting along with the crowd.

Through my sophomore and junior years, Blake kept my mind off real issues or anything deeper in life. He was my anchor, helping me weather the normal ups and downs of high school just by being there.

One Friday night in the summer before my senior year, Blake had a party at his dad's motor home by the lake. A crowd of classmates came, and the partying was going strong when I left around midnight. Blake remained at the lake.

The next day I went with him to his baseball game. On the ride home, he seemed unusually quiet. He started to say something, but didn't finish.

**My stomach churned with anger, hurt, and disgust.**

My body tensed. My heart beat faster.

"What is it?" I demanded. "Tell me!"

He just shook his head.

My mind raced through possibilities. He had been fine the night before. "What happened after I left the lake last night?"

Blake opened his mouth to speak but only swallowed.

Blake had never cheated on me or flirted with other girls. But he had never looked at me in this way before either. "Who was she?" I probed.

He named one of my teammates.

I punched him in the arm as hard as I could.

The car swerved, but Blake, still silent, righted it.

My stomach churned with anger, hurt, and disgust. After I screamed at Blake, he drove me home in silence while I cried. We were through.

I cried myself to sleep that night. But the next morning I awoke with a strong urge to go to church. I didn't understand it, but I drove to a friend's church and sat in the back alone.

The pastor's words seemed to be directed at me. I realized my life would continue beyond death because I had a soul that would never die. I could spend life after death in either heaven or hell. My choices had me pointed toward hell, but Jesus offered a way to change my destination. When the pastor invited people to come to the front of the church to pray, I went forward and admitted my sins to God, asked for forgiveness, and gave control of my life to him.

Immediately my desire for partying, drinking, doing drugs, cheating, swearing, and sleeping around ended. It's not that I thought *I can't do those things anymore.* I didn't want to do them. I had seen that the happiness those activities promised was short-lived and incomplete. Instead I wanted to read the Bible, and I began to pray. When I felt tempted to sin, I heard a voice saying, "That isn't you anymore, Sara. Turn from it."

Word got around school that I had become a "Jesus freak," but God didn't leave me abandoned. Some of my friends also had become Christians, and I drew closer to other Christians who had been praying for me for years.

Blake and I tried to mend our relationship, but he didn't understand the changes God had brought into my life. Ultimately we ended our relationship.

Turning from my old way of life and living for God wasn't always easy. But with his power and grace I never returned to it. I had a new life. I might have looked the same as my yearbook photo, but I was a different person.

*Sara L. as told to Ronica Stromberg*

# WHEN GOD
## breaks through

When our stomachs are empty, we try to fill them with whatever satisfies. When our lives are empty, we search for what satisfies as well. An earthly relationship can only satisfy for a time. But a relationship with God provides more fulfillment than we could ever imagine.

Two men living in different Old Testament time periods were inspired to give a similar message. Asaph, the writer of Psalm 81, wrote, "Open your mouth wide, and I will fill it with good things" (Psalm 81:10, NLT). Isaiah, a prophet wrote, "Come to me with your ears wide open. Listen, and you will find life" (Isaiah 55:3, NLT). The point is God is the ultimate source of satisfaction. He provides, guides, and resides within each person—filling the emptiness.

## my
## CHALLENGE

Maybe you've been where Sara was. Make a list of the people and activities you feel you can't do without. Honestly evaluate these relationships and activities. What do they add to your life? What do they take away? Are you willing to take Asaph and Isaiah's advice and turn to God?

# DEALING WITH DARKNESS 58

## overcoming **ANGER** and bitterness

*Why? Oh dear God, why?* My soul cried with the heart-rending question for months after my brother-in-law died. When someone you love dies, it's bad enough, but this was even worse: he'd taken his own life.

My oldest sister had married this man when I was only 15 and I loved him dearly. He was an accomplished trumpeter and guitarist and he played duets on the piano with my younger sister. Every day he ran six miles on the beach, and he taught me cool Frisbee games. A chemist, graduate student, and university professor, he had a marvelous mind.

He seemed to love God, even though he didn't talk about God often. I thought he was the happiest guy in the world. But at the end of the summer between my junior and senior years of high school, he decided that he'd had enough. We may never know what led him to that decision. He left us with many questions and his death changed all of our lives. My sister moved back into our home.

As I entered my senior year, I normally would have been focused on going to college. The grief was so overwhelming, however, that my college plans were put on hold as our family tried to deal with this terrible blow. Besides dealing with our own grief, each of us in the family tried especially hard to help my sister deal with her pain. We were so focused on survival that I had no room in my heart for exciting changes.

As I grieved, my friends innocently discussed their college or career goals, and my teachers reminded us to narrow our college search and fill out college applications. But I couldn't focus on college when my mind was overwhelmed with the tragedy. For the first time in my life, I felt alone and unsure of my future plans. If someone I loved so much could be gone in the blink of an eye, what about the other people I loved? Maybe they wouldn't kill themselves, but they could become sick, or be injured in an accident. There were no guarantees for anyone. Anything could happen. How could I make plans as important as college in the midst of such uncertainty?

I grew angry, thinking that my brother-in-law had ruined my senior year. I blamed the emotional stress, the delays in my college planning, having my sister back home, and my friendship troubles all on him. I was so focused on my anger that I didn't realize my parents were trying to guide me in my college choices, while struggling to console all of us. Mom looked at colleges on the Internet and asked me what kind of college I wanted to attend and what major I would consider. My dad also discussed colleges with me. But none of our hearts were in it, and I still felt resentment toward my brother-in-law.

**My brother-in-law had ruined my senior year.**

I also resented the fact that my parents now paid much less attention to me during such an important time of my life. After all, they had focused a lot on my sister when she was making college plans, and later when she made marriage plans. Now they were spending a lot of time and energy focusing on this new stage of widowhood their daughter faced.

My mom always said, "If you can't get along with your family, how can you love others?"

But my older sister and I had been at odds with each other for a long time. We're eight years apart and when she moved out, we were beginning to see eye to eye—especially since she married such a great guy. But with her sudden return to the family, our personalities clashed again. She criticized my college choices and I felt like she was picking on me.

With my older sister back home, I had to room with my younger sister. Although we usually got along well, we started competing more for my parents' limited attention. And we fought over small things, such as how to divide a room that was overly cramped and mostly mine.

Stressful relationships weren't limited to my home. Suddenly, my best friend and I were at odds. I was usually irritated and critical when she tried to discuss her college plans.

At first, I didn't realize how self-absorbed I'd become—of course it's normal for someone who's dealing with grief to think about their own pain. But I refused to let anyone help me out or take my mind off my distress and anger at the way life had changed. Besides feeling like I was in constant conflict with those around me, I began to have severe emotional breakdowns—a little more intense than people have when they're going through grief. I began to wonder what was going on in my life.

Then I started to study the book of Daniel at my church.

As I studied Daniel, chapter 4 caught my attention. King Nebuchadnezzar was proud of his stance in the world. He was so involved in his own life that he failed to realize God was in charge. But God took away his blessings and Nebuchadnezzar ended up driven out from society and became mentally ill.

I realized my emotional breakdowns didn't mean I was becoming mentally ill. And God hadn't removed my blessings—God hadn't caused or wanted my brother-in-law to take his life. But like King Nebuchadnezzar, I was totally focused on my own life. I was making my plans for great college years, and I was leaving God totally out of the equation.

Since I'd left God out of the equation when life was smooth, I was in the habit of ignoring him when circumstances weren't so good. So instead of seeking God's comfort and purpose, I focused on my anger and the unfairness of it all. When you don't deal with anger, it builds and becomes bitterness that fills your whole life.

I finally saw how bitter I had become. Those next few weeks were terrible. I just couldn't seem to let go of the pain. I felt I had a right to be bitter. After all my whole life was in upheaval. But then a speaker said, "You do not have the only situation God can't change!"

I finally realized that God was greater than my circumstances.

Yes, I'd been through a terrible situation—even though it wasn't as bad as what my older sister was going through, it was still heartbreaking, confusing, and a mess. Yes, it's normal for people to face anger and bitterness while they're dealing with grief. But there's also a time to let go, to accept life as tough as it may be, and to move on. While I was dwelling on my pain and anger, I was not reaching out to God or leaning on the support he was waiting to give me.

After that I started to look to God for the help I needed to get rid of bitterness. Part of that was learning to forgive those who had hurt me—not just my brother-in-law, but also the people who'd hurt me without meaning to, like my grieving sister and my overloaded parents.

Pride and bitterness still rear their ugly heads from time to time. I can't promise that I will be perfect, but I will try to please the God I love. Meanwhile as my life continues to change, I cling to the knowledge that no situation is out of God's hands. He may not answer all of my questions, but he loves me and will help me through all of the hard places of life.

*Andrea Howard*

## WHEN GOD
### breaks through

Unresolved anger and grief swirl together to form the funnel cloud of depression. Add bitterness and you've got a disaster waiting to happen. Andrea could see the problems her bitterness caused in her family. That's why the apostle Paul had this advice: "Get rid of all bitterness, rage and anger, brawling and slander, along with every form of malice" (Ephesians 4:31, NIV). Easier said than done? Yes. But as with any discipline, it's necessary.

### my
## CHALLENGE

Feeling angry or depressed? You're not alone. Check out these assurances of God's presence during those difficult times: Exodus 33:14; 1 Kings 19; Psalm 38:8–9.

# INVISIBLE 59

## believing that God **KNOWS** you

*God, can you even see me?* I thought as I knelt in the front of my friend's church. I felt empty, useless, like such a mess of a person. I wasn't important to anyone.

I had a Bible and I'd read it before in the privacy of my bedroom, but I never really understood it. I wanted to know more about God. I wanted to be able to understand the Bible. So when my friend had invited me to a special church program with her, I went. And when the preacher had invited people to come to the altar to pray, I went. I knelt, desperately wanting to talk to someone about my pain. I wanted to hear some kind of reassurance that at least I was important to God.

I knew enough about church to think that usually when you went to the altar, someone would join you and pray with you. And I needed help. I had no idea how to reach out to God. I waited. No one came. Not the pastor. Not even my friend.

Finally I stood. My face burning, I stumbled back to my seat feeling humiliated and emptier than before. Every eye in the church was on me, but still I felt as if I were invisible, as if no one saw who I was or the pain that was overwhelming me.

*Call me the invisible woman*, I thought.

That's how I thought of myself: invisible. Sometimes it seemed that way. I often wished I could melt into the flow of students walking in the halls. At the same time I desperately longed for someone, especially the popular kids, to notice me and talk to me.

But I wasn't the kind of girl people flocked to. For one thing, I was taller than every other girl in my class, and I had big feet to match. Even worse was my chubby figure. Academically I didn't fare any better. Although the correct answers often screamed in my head, I was too scared to raise my hand in class. I turned beet red with embarrassment if the teacher called on me.

I even wondered where my place was in our family. I had a twin brother, but he didn't share my feelings of inadequacy. We were close in many ways, but we definitely weren't alike. He didn't care about what others thought of him, and he pursued his own interests. He earned his pilot's license while most of our friends were still getting their car licenses. My "visible" twin earned the respect and pride of my parents with his extraordinary daring.

On the other hand, my extracurricular activities were about as safe as you could find. I played clarinet among a vast group in the marching band. As a senior I finally stood out as a leader in the band. This would lead me to the worst day in my life.

In Texas football is king. Every Friday morning at school our principal led a long pep rally, and by that evening our Knights were prepared to battle whatever "enemy" was on the schedule. Besides providing pep music for the fans during touchdowns and time-outs, our 90-piece band performed an elaborate halftime marching routine. It was quite a show, and we took great pride in being part of the Texas football experience.

The athletic stadium was always packed, even for the least significant high school game. At halftime one night, our band confidently marched onto the field, and the show began. I stood tall in the center of the front row next to a short sophomore boy. All went well until about the middle of the program.

The drum major's job was to blow his whistle indicating when we would begin our next maneuver, the countermarch—an impressive 180-degree turn during which each row passed through the rest of the band. The effect is that half the band is marching in the opposite direction from the other half, only inches away from each other.

This night the drum major failed to blow his whistle. Still band members were supposed to know on which yard lines to turn. And they did, except for *the sophomore boy and me.* Eighty-eight musicians were swiftly heading away from us, and we couldn't do anything about it.

I was horrified, but I remembered what our director had told us to do in such a predicament: make a 90-degree turn and march off the field as if it were a planned maneuver. Since I was the upperclassman in the situation, I told my companion we would turn at the next yard line and exit the field.

At the next yard line, though, he turned right and I turned left, and we collided. Hard. I quickly turned him around and off we marched, humiliated, to the visiting team's sideline. Not only had we messed up on the field, but now we had to walk around the field to our own sideline! Suddenly I wished I was invisible!

My faux pas didn't make much of a ripple at my large high school, but it destroyed my last shred of self-confidence.

That's when I turned again to God in earnest. Surely if anyone could help restore my sagging self-confidence, God could. Surely he cared. This time I asked for help from my Christian friend. I felt reassured that God *had* seen me at the altar on the night when no one had come to talk to me. She explained that my growing desire to obey God, combined with the guiding of the Holy Spirit, demonstrated that God truly knew me.

He had always known about me and cared.

I started to realize that God loved sometimes klutzy, often unnoticed, me! I began to grow deeper in my faith as I read my Bible, went to church, and hung

**Eighty-eight musicians were swiftly heading away from us, and we couldn't do anything about it.**

out with other believers. Slowly my whole life began to change. As I grew confident that God actually loved me, I started worrying less about what others thought. As a result I stopped trying to be so invisible, and let myself participate in life. For example, with my increased faith and confidence, I could raise my hand in class to answer a question. Later that year I even won a clarinet competition, even though performing in front of judges was scary.

As I read the Bible, I found I could understand it. God led me to a passage which encouraged me: "Forgetting what is behind and straining toward what is ahead, I press on toward the goal to win the prize for which God has called me heavenward in Christ Jesus" (Philippians 3:13–14, NIV).

This passage reminded me that I had a clean slate with God. I didn't have to worry about my halftime performance (or lack thereof); I could quit worrying about mistakes and keep my eyes focused on what God has in store for me in the future.

I don't care if I'm invisible or way too visible—as long as God sees me!

*Barbara Lewis*

# WHEN GOD
## breaks through

Ever feel completely invisible to those around you? This can happen when you feel misunderstood. Or perhaps you've also encountered times—embarrassing times—when you wish you *were* invisible. David, the writer of Psalm 139, took comfort in the fact that the God of the universe saw and understood him at all times. "O LORD, you have searched me and you know me. You know when I sit and when I rise; you perceive my thoughts from afar. You discern my going out and my lying down; you are familiar with all my ways" (Psalm 139:1–3, NIV). Does that comfort you?

## my
## CHALLENGE

Reeling from a misunderstanding or an embarrassing event? Remember that God is always present and perfectly understands your situation. Contemplate on Psalm 139:1–3 and rewrite it in your own words.

# learning to **LAUGH** at oneself

It was one of those days. First thing in the morning, I accidentally bumped into a cheerleader entering biology class. She glared at me. Then when I came out of the bathroom after lunch, I didn't realize the back of my skirt was caught in my underwear. And as I started down the hall, that same cheerleader led the whole school in mocking me.

I ran back to the bathroom feeling like a complete moron. If only I could just disappear!

Staring at my scarlet reflection in the mirror, I reviewed my failures. Even though I wrote for the school's newspaper, I wasn't among the popular kids. I was always on the outside, asking questions, looking into other people's lives, never really fitting in.

On top of that, I had fallen in love with Urs, the exchange student from Switzerland, after I interviewed him for the paper. But he was out of my league. He was handsome, on the football team, and radiated a calm confidence in God. And he was dating Cheryl, the very cheerleader who hated me!

"Please get me through this day, Lord," I prayed. Then I braced myself to return to the hallway.

Thankfully the crowd had dispersed.

I didn't run into Cheryl again until later in the day when I decided to take a shortcut across the student parking lot to my last class. Cheryl and her crowd had gathered around a car, laughing again. But at least this time I wasn't the brunt of their joke.

As I got a bit closer, I realized they were writing in the frost on the windows of a senior's car. But Cheryl was pointing at Urs, her boyfriend, as she laughed. Apparently he was writing the German word for love, *liebe*, on the car. So what did Cheryl think was so funny about that? He used his middle finger to write in the frost.

To Urs it was just a finger. He didn't have a clue why that was a cause for humor. And that made the kids laugh even more.

Urs looked over the crowd of kids at me. The silly grin on his face said, "OK. I see the joke is on me and I don't care. Just somebody tell me the joke please?"

But no one did. They just mimicked Urs's use of that finger.

Urs shrugged his shoulders, waved goodbye to the group, and headed straight for me.

"I am pretty funny, eh?" he said.

"Yes, you're funny and cute. But they aren't," I said pointing behind him. Cheryl stood with her mouth open.

**To Urs it was just a finger. He didn't have a clue why that was a cause for humor.**

Urs shrugged again. "They laugh *at* people, not *with* people. You like to laugh *with* me."

He suddenly hugged me, and I felt as if I was soaring to heaven! In that moment I knew God was challenging me not to give up hope and not to turn everything that happened into a tragedy!

I realized if Cheryl hadn't been someone who mocked people, Urs might have stayed with her! Instead he stopped dating her and asked me out instead.

Urs and I spent lots of time together before he returned to Switzerland. While we were together, I learned to laugh at myself and to turn problems over to God.

When I forgot an assignment, when I embarrassed myself, when I made a mistake, Urs shrugged and laughed. "It'll all work out. Just smile. Have faith that God is with you," he would say.

In a few short months I felt lighter. I began to pray, "Lord, help me keep laughing." And I knew that he would help me with that and a whole lot more.

*Judith Costello*

# WHEN GOD
## breaks through

Urs helped Judith see the value of laughter and trusting in God. Are both important to you? Learning to laugh at yourself starts with knowing yourself and God, as the apostle Paul suggests. "Don't think you are better than you really are. Be honest in your evaluation of yourselves, measuring yourselves by the faith God has given us. . . . Rejoice in our confident hope" (Romans 12:3, 12, NLT). As you rejoice in your hope in God, you can't help but laugh.

## my
## CHALLENGE

Do you have difficulty laughing at yourself? Consider asking God for the humility to see your situation through his eyes. Ask a close friend to assess your ability to laugh at yourself. Maybe that person can help pinpoint situations you might have taken too seriously. Note these, and the next time a potentially embarrassing situation comes up, take time to pray that God will help you see the lighter side.

## asking for **HELP** in tough times

"Hey, Tim, guess what happened this week!"

"Yo, Mr. T, check this out."

"Hey, I wanted to sit there!"

Chaos reigns as 20 kids try to talk to me at once, 20 squabble over their seats or other inane things, and another 20 talk to their friends at full volume, trying to be heard above the din. And add to that up to 10 kids just sitting quietly, trying to take it all in.

This is my life every Saturday—on a bus in Richmond, taking rowdy inner-city kids to church at the Richmond Outreach Center to hear a message of hope.

It's hard to believe that just four years ago, I was one of these kids.

I was 14 when I met the ROC's youth pastor, Ronnie Ortiz, on my way to play basketball. Being stopped on the street by a guy with such a tough look and tattooed neck usually meant trouble in my neighborhood, but he only wanted to tell me how to accept Christ as my Lord and Savior.

I had nothing going for me and I knew I had to try something. My father had left us when I was two. My mom and stepfather had their struggles, and the street life was beginning to affect my brother and sister.

After praying with Ronnie I got excited about God and began to serve him at the ROC. At least I tried to serve him. I attended a city school and was a pretty good student and athlete, but the atmosphere challenged me. People could talk about sex and fighting all they wanted, but to mention Jesus meant trouble. So I didn't talk about Jesus much. I figured I could still hang out with my non-Christian friends and not become like them. But over time I fell into all their behaviors. This frustrated me. So in my junior year, I dropped out of school, thinking I could just serve God full time.

The head pastor at the ROC, Geronimo Aguilar, had come out of the Los Angeles gangs. When I told him I dropped out of school, he said, "Always finish what you start, Tim." He arranged for me to attend a Christian school and play basketball for them.

Although my school life got better, my home life was hard. My family drank and smoked, and my brother and sister were getting involved in drugs. Mom struggled with depression—and with me. She felt a lot of anger toward me because I reminded her of my father who used to beat her before they divorced. I'm even Tim Junior.

A couple of times I moved out and then moved back in again, trying to make things work. My last attempt to live at home fell apart because I was too judgmental about their lifestyles. I criticized them instead of just loving them and trying to show them Jesus through my love. The next thing I knew, they wanted me gone and I wanted to be gone.

**The next thing I knew, they wanted me gone and I wanted to be gone.**

Once again I ended up on the streets, but this time it was my senior year—the biggest year of my life. I was still playing basketball at the Christian school and at the end of practice, I had nowhere to go. The coach would tell everyone it was time to leave and I'd say, "I'm waiting on my ride." When he left I jumped on a bus used only for sports teams in the warm season and stayed on the empty bus at night.

For five weeks in November and December, I lived on that bus in the parking lot of the school, showering in the school locker room when the janitor unlocked the door early in the morning. At night I slept in layers of clothes, sprawled across the bus seats. Miss Cousins, the cafeteria lady, gave me food because I didn't have money to buy lunch.

At any point I could've asked those people for help, and God kept telling me to tell someone—Pastor G or anyone—but it was embarrassing enough to have to accept free meals. I was 18 years old and felt I didn't need anyone but God.

Then my body began to shut down. I was exhausted in school, and people started to notice something was wrong. One night I realized I could no longer go to the bathroom.

That scared me. But still I didn't want to admit to anyone that I needed help. Finally I prayed, "All right, God. I can't do it anymore. I'm sorry. You know me. I'm just so proud and scared to ask for help. Please do something."

The next day God answered that prayer when I was called to the school office. One of my coaches stood there with a black bag of clothes and said, "Tim, are these yours?" Someone had gone onto the bus and found my stuff.

"Yeah, those are mine."

"Have you been living on that bus?"

"Yeah."

"For how long?"

"Well, about five weeks."

"Let's talk," he said. He took me to the principal and I told them about being asked to leave my house.

Miss Cousins took me into her home—no questions asked. I was pleased to have a roof over my head, and was especially happy that I would get some good meals. But when I tried to down Miss Cousins' good food, I couldn't eat. My body rejected everything I tried to consume. It was so broken down that I had to start with applesauce and fluids before I worked up to a sandwich.

Eventually Miss Cousins told me that God is a God of restoration. She encouraged me to have short conversations with my mother. Mom and I didn't talk about anything serious—just how we loved each other. Slowly our relationship healed. By the time graduation rolled around, we had seen each other a couple of times. Eventually my family started attending church.

Right after graduation the ROC bought my Christian school's property and Pastor G surprised me by asking me to move into a discipleship home on their grounds and serve with them. I was in full-time ministry! Even better, my family kept healing. My brother later moved into the same discipleship home and my sister got involved with InterVarsity when she went to college.

Before I'd been at the discipleship home for long, Pastor G asked me to be a part of the Whosoever Bus Ministry that picks up kids for church.

*Are you kidding? I don't want to get back on a bus!* I thought at first. Those five weeks had discouraged me from buses for life. But then I thought of the kids who needed my help. Kids I could understand because I'd been there.

So now every Saturday I go to this rough neighborhood on the south side of Richmond. I try to listen to them above the din, and tease them, and show them they are loved. And all the while I'm watching them and praying and looking for ways to help—especially among the kids who are too proud to ask for it. Their situations may look hard and they may even feel hopeless, but the same God who rescued me can rescue them.

*Tim M. as told to Linda MacKillop*

## WHEN GOD
### breaks through

Some situations are so difficult, we're embarrassed to tell anyone about them. Can you relate? That's the way Tim's life was. But he eventually discovered a truth the apostle Peter expressed in his first letter: "Humble yourselves, therefore, under God's mighty hand, that he may lift you up in due time" (1 Peter 5:6, CEV). We may balk at humbling ourselves, but in the long run it's worth it to accept the help we need.

### my
## CHALLENGE

Do you have any areas in your life in which you need help, but you're a little too embarrassed to ask for it? Today ask God to help you find the strength to talk to someone about your situation.

## waiting for **GOD'S** choice

What excuse would it be this time?

"Um, I'm kind of busy this weekend."

"I'm really not looking for a boyfriend right now."

"I have to wash my hair that day."

Right up into my senior year, those were the answers I always heard from girls when I proposed a date. OK, I made that last one up. I never really heard it. But I heard the others enough that I was tempted to just simplify the process and offer girls a multiple-choice list when I called.

The conversation would go like this:

"Hi, uh, Kelli? This is David. Would you like to go out on Friday?"

I'd pause to see if she'd actually say yes. Then with a heavy sigh I'd say, "Your choices are:

"A. My parents won't let me date.

"B. My weekends are taken up through my senior year.

"C. I'm allergic to teenage boys' cars.

"D. Can't we just be friends?"

Based on my experience, D was the most popular choice.

Just about every girl I met wanted my friendship, but not romance, including the girl I took to the junior prom. The trend seemed unlikely to stop.

I quizzed myself: Is it that I'm cute, not handsome? I've got money and a car. Do I smell bad? Most girls didn't even move within sniffing range before rejecting my offer of a simple date. Maybe I wasn't smooth enough. I had to admit I stumbled over my words and became flustered when I approached girls with romantic intent. At other times, when there was no chance of romance, I *was* their friend. I could be witty, give comfort, and make them feel special.

Of course I realized romantic relationships could include their share of misery. None of my female friends had ever treated me as badly as they had treated their boyfriends at times. Some of my dating friends had become pregnant and married. Seeing the realistic side of dating though, never really took away the sting of each rejection.

One night I pondered these things as I got ready for bed. Then I prayed as I drifted off to sleep. "God, please help me get a date. But I still yield to your will. I don't understand it, but I guess none of these girls have been right for me."

**I quizzed myself: Is it that I'm cute, not handsome?…maybe I wasn't smooth enough.**

The next day I got up late and skipped breakfast as usual. Band went well. I talked to Kelli who had rejected me with a note on Sunday during church. She was having problems with others in the flute section and just needed to vent her frustrations to someone.

Margaret needed help in math, and I obliged. She'd been dating the same guy since the day she arrived at my high school. But what did that matter if she needed help in math and I could give it? Still she was pretty and I would have asked for a date—if she didn't already have a boyfriend. Wait! I think I actually did ask her out once when she and her boyfriend had split, but then they made up.

In chemistry, Toni failed another test. She wasn't dumb, she just didn't do well in science. I offered a study session at my house. She jumped at the chance and hugged me. *If I had a girlfriend,* I thought, *I could get hugs like that all the time.* And yes, I'd asked Toni out for a date in the past. The result was the usual: answer D.

Later Haven, my buddy's girlfriend, was having trouble with him and wanted to talk to me about it. She didn't want me to fix it; she just needed someone to listen and understand. And I did. I didn't understand why she didn't just talk to her boyfriend, but she needed a listening ear so I didn't even think about her as a prospective date. It would hurt my friend, and it probably wouldn't work anyway.

For the rest of my senior year, I continued to pray for success with girls, but each time I added that I wanted God's will to be done in my life. I wished I could have left that last part out of my prayers, but God's Spirit wouldn't leave me alone until I added it.

I saw the answer to that prayer clearly a few days before I left for college when I read the notes written in my senior yearbook:

*I'll miss you and your special friendship. Kelli.*

*I'm really going to miss you. You really helped me make it through a hard year. Margaret.*

*You mean so much to me! Thanks for all your help and advice with school, all my troubles. I owe you a lot. Toni.*

*You've been a great friend and you always made me laugh when I was depressed. I'm going to miss your friendly smile. Haven.*

I realized my friendships with girls were more significant to me and them than any high school romance could ever have been.

*David W. Barnett*

# WHEN GOD
## breaks through

When major decisions loom on the horizon, in what or whom do you trust? The advice of your friends or family? Self-help books? The prophet Isaiah reminds us that God is a constant source of guidance: "The Lord will guide you always; he will satisfy your needs" (Isaiah 58:11, NIV). Best of all, he's available 24/7. Sometimes God's guidance comes in the form of a timely passage out of the Bible. Other times you might hear good advice from a godly friend or family member.

## my
## CHALLENGE

What are you waiting for? The right date? The right college or after-school job? Have you asked God for his input on the decisions that face you? Make a list of the ways God has spoken to you this week through the advice of a friend or parent, through the Scriptures you've heard, or through other means.

## persisting in **FAITH**

I always said I trusted God, but that belief was shaken when I tried out for the volleyball team. Ever since I first gave my heart to Jesus as a little girl, I believed he would always answer my prayers. And the summer I was 13, all I wanted was to be part of that volleyball team.

My school in Swannanoa, North Carolina, was known for its winning girls' volleyball program. The team members were quick, powerful, and popular. Their record was impressive; even their new uniforms were perfect. So I set my sights on the coming fall season, prayed, and worked toward the goal of joining the team with all my strength. I was confident God would help me reach my goal.

That summer I spent hours perfecting my passes, hits, and serves in our backyard. Three times a week I attended "open gym" run by the coaches at school. I lived and breathed volleyball, and my skills steadily improved.

Soon summer was over and it was time for tryouts. My friends and I sweated through two days of drills before the watchful eyes of coaches carrying clipboards. Finally it was time for the team to be announced. I chatted happily with other girls and waited for my name to be called. One by one my friends stood and joined the teammates on the bleachers. I waited and waited, but my moment never came. I was not chosen.

My eyes filled with tears and my throat tightened. I just wanted to get away from my successful friends. I felt totally humiliated.

After the initial shock I got really mad. How could God do this to me? Hadn't he noticed my hard work? He could have answered my prayers to make the team; it was such a small thing to ask. Didn't God have better things to do than to crush a young girl's hopes? I felt as if I'd been run over by a truck.

For a week I grieved. Then as I talked to my parents and opened my broken heart to God again, I made a decision: I was tired of feeling sorry for myself. It was time to do something new. I really wanted to be on an athletic team, but the only other fall sport was cross country track. I didn't know if I could run a mile without stopping, but I decided to try.

On the first day of practice, only three of us showed up. More kids gradually joined our ranks until we had the minimum needed for a team. We didn't need to pass high-powered tryouts—we just had to have running shoes, a water bottle, and the willingness to work hard. We met every day in humid weather, running laps around the parking lot because our school had no track. Some days we ran up hills. Some days we ran sprints. We ran and ran and ran.

Our coach believed in us. As she trained us she also taught us to encourage each other. Stretching exercises, daily runs, and meets all became opportunities for us to spur each other toward excellence. Runners who finished a race first would go back and accompany the slower runners during the final leg. We didn't take top honors, but we all got faster and stronger. We didn't have many cheering fans, but we were a team.

Those few months of running on the cross country team taught me lessons I could not have learned otherwise. For one thing, I learned a lot about endurance. Many times I

**I waited and waited, but my moment never came. I was not chosen.**

gasped for breath, tempted to give up, yet I found the strength to press on to the finish line.

In volleyball the star players usually get more time on the court than the second-stringers, but cross-country has no benchwarmers. Everyone runs the same race. Realizing this made me respect my fellow runners, no matter how fast or slow they were. I became eager to cheer for them instead of just thinking about my own race.

I think the most important thing I learned didn't have anything to do with running, but with trusting God. Playing volleyball had been my heart's desire, but God had different goals for me that year, and he worked through my bitter disappointment to accomplish them. This is important because I frequently face disappointments. Some are everyday things, like failing a tough math test even though I studied. Others are major, like watching my grandmother die of cancer while I prayed for her to live. Struggles and losses don't mean God doesn't care. His hopes and dreams for my life—and for those I love—are bigger and better than what I can see. He uses everything that comes my way to shape me into the person he created me to be.

The more I comprehend that truth, the surer I become of God's unshakable love for me. Knowing that love, I can dare to trust him completely. No matter what.

*Anna S. as told to Ruth Ann Somerville*

## WHEN GOD
### breaks through

Instead of giving up, Anna chose to push past disappointment. This is basically what the apostle Paul told the believers in the city of Philippi:

> *I have not yet reached my goal, and I am not perfect. But Christ has taken hold of me. So I keep on running and struggling to take hold of the prize. My friends, I don't feel that I have already arrived. But I forget what is behind, and I struggle for what is ahead. I run toward the goal, so that I can win the prize of being called to heaven. . . . We must keep going in the direction that we are now headed (Philippians 3:12–16, CEV).*

Paul knew that the Christian life is a race to the finish. Although "everyone runs the same race," as Anna suggested, we don't all run in the same way. But we can encourage each other to endure.

### my
## CHALLENGE

Feeling stalled by disappointment, or know someone who is? If you keep a journal, write a description of where you are right now or talk with a friend about what's happening in his or her life. Take time to ask God to help you see other options.

# A MATTER OF PERSPECTIVE 64

## finding God in **REAL** life

"Hey teacher, José likes you. He thinks you're cute."

A burst of laughter drowned out my voice as I struggled to control the class.

*Teacher!* I felt a spasm of panic. I regretted my agreement to lead children's church, which was quickly turning into a fiasco. I was 18 years old and one of the few young people left in a fast-declining church of mainly elderly people. I quickly realized that just being young didn't necessarily qualify me to teach young kids.

Being young definitely seemed to work against me. The kids took advantage of my age and were talking out loud and throwing papers. I tried to regain my composure and started to read a story from the curriculum I had been given. The story was about saying "no" to temptation. But the lesson plan had a picture of a Caucasian boy with a 1950s crew cut who was struggling about whether to disobey his mother and steal a cookie from the cookie jar. It was totally irrelevant and outdated. Most of the kids were Latino and hardly saw their mothers who had little time to be with the family, let alone make cookies. I could understand why they didn't want to hear a story about something they couldn't relate to.

I was at a turning point as well. I went to church because it was the right thing to do, but could not sense God there. The people seemed out of touch with reality just like the lesson I was teaching. I had nearly decided to leave and not come back, but then I was assigned this class.

*Just six more weeks,* I thought, *and then I'm out of here.*

I looked at the kids again—at their insolent attitudes—and suddenly saw myself. I believed in God, but in my own way.

A sudden inspiration seized me. "Give me those handouts," I said, grimacing at the outdated papers. I grabbed one that had a mustache drawn on Johnny's face. The kids giggled.

"Do you know any boys like this?" I asked. "No? Neither do I." I threw the handouts in the trash.

The kids got quiet and I whispered to one of the older kids to go to the nursery and get some things for me.

"Look," I said, "I know you don't relate to this right now and neither do I. So we are just going to talk about what's real. This book called the Bible is about real people dealing with real problems. I have real problems. A girl I know got

> **"Look," I said, "I know you don't relate to this right now and neither do I."**

pregnant at 13 and her mom kicked her out. I didn't know what to say to her, so I read the Bible and it told me. My house got robbed three times and left me so scared I couldn't sleep at night. So I prayed. I asked God to help me and he did."

By this time the girl I sent to the nursery returned with a Ken doll, a car, a dollhouse, a boy doll, a girl doll, and a stuffed dragon. The kids laughed, but I knew I had their complete attention. I opened the Bible and read 1 Corinthians 10:13 (*The Living Bible*):

> *Remember this—the wrong desires that come into your life aren't anything new and different. Many others have faced exactly the same problems before you. And no temptation is irresistible. You can trust God to keep the temptation from becoming so strong that you can't stand up against it, for he has promised this and will do what he says. He will show you how to escape temptation's power so that you can bear up patiently against it.*

"Let's talk about some real issues," I said. "These toys will help. This is

Satan." I pointed to the dragon. "Except he is invisible and is roaming around trying to get people to do bad things. The Ken doll represents temptation because he is the person who tries to get you to do bad things. I will pretend to be God because I am in charge of the situation and making the dolls move."

The kids were mesmerized as I created a scenario where the boy doll was being tempted to make a lot of money by selling something in a paper bag. As the dragon whispered in his ear and the tempter (Ken doll) tried to sell him the goods, the sister (the girl doll) called him to come home. I stopped and asked the kids where the way out of the temptation was for the boy.

"The girl!" they shouted.

After that the kids nearly taught themselves. I had them reenact some of the temptations they wrote on the board, and then we talked about ways of escape. Soon they were talking about other issues.

"I saw my dad hit my mom," one girl said.

"My brother is in a gang!" another shouted.

They seemed to find great relief in talking about the reality of their situations. At the end of class I had the kids all pray for each other. I told them God would help them and knew their situations. They could find the answers in the Bible.

Before I knew it, the class was over. I felt a new exhilaration. God *was* real and had spoken just as clearly to me as to those kids. My perspective changed and so did my life.

*Colleen J. Yang*

# WHEN GOD
## breaks through

Ever hear someone question whether God is real? Perhaps those words came out of your mouth. Or perhaps you've wondered whether believing in God is important today. After all times change, right? Times may change, but God does not. The writer of Hebrews explained it this way: "Jesus Christ is the same yesterday, today, and forever" (Hebrews 13:8, NLT). His plans, rules, and words remain the same. That means no matter what happens, God will always be there for you. Knowing this changed Colleen's perspective. Does it change yours?

## my
## CHALLENGE

What is your perspective of God? Does he seem real? Far away? If you journal, write your thoughts on this. Consider Hebrews 13:8. If God seems far away, check out Psalms 106:4 and 119:51. Ask God to help you sense his presence.

## learning to be a **LEADER**

"The things that are going on in our church just aren't right," I said to my mom after church while we were eating lunch at the mall.

Our denomination had recently been in the news as having an openly gay bishop. People in the denomination disagreed in their opinions about this. I thought it was wrong for practicing homosexuals to serve as pastors, and now our church was at a crossroads. Our pastor had just retired and the church needed to find a replacement.

"I'm worried about who might come in," I said. "Sometimes I wish I were a little older so I could do something about these problems. I wish I could be on the search committee."

A few days later a member of our vestry, or church council, called our house. "Bobby, would you be interested in serving as a youth representative for the search committee?" she asked.

*Whoa,* I thought, *that's incredible. Who would have thought that would happen?*

The church could have easily chosen to exclude youth from taking part in the pastoral search. As a junior, I was the only high school student active at my church. The next oldest kids were in junior high. The fact that the vestry invited me, and so quickly after I said I wished I could take part, seemed more than coincidence.

"Thank you for asking me," I said, "but let me talk it over with my parents first."

I told my parents about the phone call. They were as surprised as I was because neither had told anyone about my comment at the mall.

"Well," Mom said, "you said you wanted to be on the search committee. Here's your chance."

"All right," I said. "I'll take it."

When we gathered for the first time, we created a parish profile to tell candidates about our church and its basic statistics. Then the congregation met in an open forum to list the qualities they wanted in a pastor. Some people wanted a pastor with a sense of humor, others wanted someone who was good with kids. Still others wanted someone who could preach well.

I stood and said, "We could go on all day listing what we want to see in a pastor, but in the end, what do those things mean? The important part is that we have somebody who wants to prepare and nurture people in God's church."

**"Well," Mom said, "you said you wanted to be on the search committee. Here's your chance."**

As I said this I realized that the youth had the most to gain or lose in any decisions about the future of our church. In the decades to come, we would be living with the decisions made.

Since the open forum the search committee has tried to meet twice a month. We are at the beginning of the search process, still needing to send out a brochure and interview pastors. This could take a long time, but I'm committed to representing the youth as I was called to do. I still haven't had the chance to speak about the homosexuality issue, but when the time is right I will, because it's something my church needs to face.

So far people on the search committee and in my church seem to value my opinion. Some people may not expect me to care about the homosexual issue. They might think that as the youth representative, I'm searching for a pastor to get more social activities going for youth or build a better youth room. But

I think the best thing the church can do for the youth—and the congregation as a whole—is to give them sound, biblical leadership.

My work on the search committee has given me confidence and helped me see my part in the future of the church. And that's something for teenagers to practice everywhere.

*Bobby B. as told to Ronica Stromberg*

## WHEN GOD
### breaks through

If you've wondered whether your voice counts, consider some advice the apostle Paul had for Timothy, a young pastor who struggled with being a leader: "Don't let anyone make fun of you, just because you are young. Set an example for other followers by what you say and do, as well as by your love, faith, and purity" (1 Timothy 4:12, CEV). Although some may not applaud your leadership efforts, are you willing to take a stand anyway?

## my
## CHALLENGE

Even if you don't have the opportunity to serve on a church search committee, you can still be a leader. What are some opportunities you have to exercise your leadership potential? This might involve simply being a role model to younger students.

# A POOLSIDE CHAT 66

## coming **ALONGSIDE** a friend

School was finally out for summer. For the past three years I had been a lifeguard and swim teacher at a city pool, so I was ready for another summer of fun, sun, and poolside chats with friends while keeping watch over the little ones splashing around in the pool.

This summer would be a bit more challenging, however. I was named the pool manager. *Wow,* I thought, *pool manager at age eighteen—I must be doing something right!* As manager I was responsible for added duties: teaching swim lessons, lifeguarding during pool hours, setting the schedule for the other lifeguards, and collecting pool entrance money and depositing it in the bank downtown at the close of the day. I also had to train and supervise the crew of lifeguards.

I had a great crew to work with. I knew all the guards from the previous summer. Plus there was a new girl, Sallie. She was a little quieter than the rest of the group, but she was a great worker and loved to have fun—just like me.

As the summer went on, Sallie and I became good friends. She didn't have a car, so I would take her to and from work every day.

Toward the middle of the summer, the lifeguards were getting excited about a big rock concert coming into town featuring the hottest group at that time. While they were excitedly making plans to go, I was juggling schedules, trying to let those off who requested to go.

The concert day came and the buzz among the guards was palpable. Sallie could hardly contain herself as this was her favorite band. The guards were excited to clock out a little early, and as they left I have to admit I was jealous. On that particular afternoon, being the manager carried a responsibility that I would have gladly traded for a ticket to the concert.

I began swimming lessons early the next day, eagerly waiting to hear how the concert went. As I finished up my last beginner's class, I could hear the phone ringing in the office. Toweling off quickly, I ran to pick it up.

"Hello?" I panted, half out of breath.

"May I speak with the manager?" a quiet, deep voice asked.

"This is she."

"This is Sallie's dad. I haven't met you, but, um . . . she spoke very kindly of you. I need to let you know . . . she was killed in a car accident last night."

**"Sallie was hit head-on by a drunk driver last night after the concert."**

"Excuse me?" Did my ears still have water in them?

"Sallie was hit head-on by a drunk driver last night after the concert. I will be by the pool this afternoon to pick up her belongings."

"Yes, sir. I'm so sorry."

Hanging up the phone I felt paralyzed. How was I going to tell the other guards? How was I going to face her dad when he came to get her things? My mind was racing, yet I felt numb and speechless. I never imagined this responsibility when I took over as manager. I began to pray that God would give me strength to cope with the tragedy. I knew I could not make it through alone.

As the guards strolled in to work, sharing the news of Sallie's death was harder than I had thought. We all sat in disbelief, reminiscing about Sallie's days and how we'd come to love her quirky little smile. I felt especially unprepared to see her dad. I had never lost a friend before; it all seemed like a dream—a horrible dream.

As children and families began to come in to swim, the news passed around. Questions were coming from every corner in the pool. All I wanted to do was leave and mourn for Sallie in my own private way. I continued praying, God please help me through this day.

Sitting in the guard stand watching the children splash and play, I felt a gentle touch on my shoulder. Glancing over I saw Keith. Keith and I had gone to church together since we were five, and he had become like a big brother who always watched after me. He told me he had heard the news and knew I must be having a hard time. Had God heard my prayer and answered that quickly? He must have. Keith was the answer to my prayers.

I was comforted by his tender spirit and the reassurance that he would not leave my side calmed my weary heart. When I was on the guard stand, Keith sat on the side of the pool beside me. When I was in the office taking money, he was in the office as well, welcoming those who came to swim.

Toward the end of the afternoon, a man dressed in a nice suit walked up to the pool area. Though we had never met, I knew immediately he was Sallie's dad and began muttering under my breath, "I can't do this. I can't do this."

Keith assured me that he would be with me. He reminded me that I had prayed for strength and God was answering that prayer. When I choked up, Keith handed him Sallie's belongings and escorted him to his car.

Keith returned and we prayed together, asking God for comfort and strength. My friend's presence reminding me that God would give me strength is what helped me through the tough responsibilities on that sad summer day. Keith showed me the true meaning of friendship when he canceled what he had planned and spent the day with me. God demonstrated that he answers prayers and often he does that by sending a friend like Keith.

*Alene Snodgrass*

# WHEN GOD
## breaks through

You've heard the old saying, "A friend in need is a friend in deed." But a proverb with a similar message is "There are 'friends' who destroy each other, but a real friend sticks closer than a brother" (Proverbs 18:24, NLT). Keith proved himself to be a loyal friend to Alene—one who was there just when she needed him. This kind of friend isn't out for what he or she can get. Instead this friend is quick to offer help and to show love.

## my
## CHALLENGE

Who are the friends you count on to help you through tough times? Find some way to express your gratitude to them—either with a small gift, an offer to go for coffee, or a heartfelt thank you. Let someone else know that you are there for them.

# NOT FINISHED YET 67

## crying out to **GOD** when he's all you have left

How does an apparently normal family come apart overnight? I will tell you.

It happened when I was a high school sophomore. First, Dad left. He told my mom he was having an affair and was leaving. On his way out he stopped in the kitchen where I was eating dinner with my sister and little brother. He was tired of being our father, he said, as if it were no big deal. He was leaving.

The slamming front door felt like a punch in the stomach. My brother started to cry and my sister ran upstairs to see Mom, but I just sat there, not believing what had just happened.

A few days later Mom announced that she needed some space to figure out her life. She packed a suitcase and told my sister and me to take care of our brother. Then she headed out the door with a promise to call us when she got to wherever she was going.

I stood in the front hall staring at my sister and brother, wondering how God could do nothing while our lives fell more and more apart.

Mom came home a few days at a time, only to leave again. Dad called occasionally and dropped off money at the house while we were at school. My sister wouldn't let us tell anyone outside our family what was happening. She was convinced our parents would work it out and she thought it would be embarrassing for them if they had to explain to our friends or people at church what happened. So we simply tried to go on without any parents. My sister and I made dinner, did the laundry, helped our brother with homework, and kept the household running.

But I couldn't go even an hour without feeling physical pain when I thought about my dad walking out and my mom running away. Who cared if they were tired or lost? They were the parents! How could they leave us completely on our own?

More important, how could God turn his back on us?

The weeks wore on and my sister and I began to fight. The pain, uncertainty, fear,

**"GOD! I am done with you! Go away! I don't need you anymore!"**

stress, and loneliness were just too much and we took it out on each other. After one big blowup, I grabbed my coat and walked into the cold night. It was late, but I didn't care. I had to get out. Crying, I just walked, unaware of anything going on around me. I had never felt so empty and alone. I ended up a mile from home in the middle of my high school's football field.

"GOD!" I yelled. "Where are you? How could you do this to me? What did I do to make you leave me and my family? Don't you love me anymore?"

Then louder than before, I yelled, "GOD! I am done with you! Go away! I don't need you anymore!"

I crumbled to the ground and lay on my back staring at the stars. The grass was damp, but I didn't care. I was spent. I was done with God, my family, life. I was completely alone. And that was what I wanted, because I was pretty sure that once you yelled at God and told him to go away, he wouldn't come back.

Then a little voice said, "Are you finished?"

Was someone else on the field? I squinted in the darkness and looked around, but saw no one.

"Are you finished?" I heard again.

My heart beat faster. I had heard people at church talk about literally hearing God, but I had never believed it. Could God really be talking to me? I sat in silence, wondering if I would hear the voice again.

As I waited I started to cry and I felt God's presence like never before. And then the small voice said, "Can I prove to you how much you can trust me?"

In that moment my anger subsided. "God," I said quietly, "if you are really here talking to me, please show me how to rely on you. I am not sure you are here, but if you are you are all I have left."

It would be nice to say God fixed everything in that moment, but he didn't. Too many hard days followed. My parents didn't get back together; in fact some of my worst moments were watching my parents fight over who got what in their divorce. But in the midst of it all, God proved to me that I could trust him. He provided incredible people to love me back to life and help me to see that my parents' breakup was not my fault. He healed my heart.

Since that night on the football field, God has never let me down. I may have been finished with God on that night, but God certainly wasn't finished with me.

*Molly as told to Nina Edwards*

# WHEN GOD
## breaks through

People sometimes talk about "hitting bottom"—reaching life's lowest ebb. Some situations in life can strip your emotions raw. Can't you sense the agony David the psalmist and king of Israel felt as he wrote, "My God, my God, why have you abandoned me? Why are you so far away when I groan for help? Every day I call to you, my God, but you do not answer. Every night you hear my voice, but I find no relief" (Psalm 22:1–3, NLT).

Many centuries later Jesus screamed these same words while in agony on the cross. Although we may feel abandoned by God in our pain, Jesus truly experienced God's rejection. But the psalm doesn't end there. "Yet you are holy, enthroned on the praises of Israel. Our ancestors trusted in you, and you rescued them" (Psalm 22:4, NLT). Agony gave way to an acknowledgment of God's presence and character. Molly experienced this.

When you're in agony, consider the Savior who experienced true abandonment so you'll never have to. He knows how you feel.

my
# CHALLENGE

Talk with God or with a trusted friend or family member about a hard experience you're going through. Try not to cover or downplay your feelings. Be real.

# AUTHOR BIOS

**Allison Asimakoupoulos** is studying early childhood education and creative writing at North Park University in Chicago. She grew up in Naperville, Illinois, with two sisters. Along with writing, Allison enjoys scrapbooking, trying out new recipes, and has a slight fascination with pirates.

**David W. Barnett** lives in Arlington, Texas, with his wife and three daughters. When he's not working or playing with his children, he enjoys teaching at his church and writing.

**Kelsey Berry** is a student at Griffith High School. She lives with her parents and three siblings. She enjoys playing soccer and piano.

**Marija Birchard** is from Wheaton, Illinois. Currently she is attending the College of DuPage and majoring in journalism. She enjoys hanging out with her friends, reading, and watching movies.

**Mike Brantley** leads a mission community, La Communauté, in New Orleans. He and his wife, Susanne, are on staff with Church Resource Ministries, in Communitas, which is focused on reaching the vast number of people beyond the geography of the existing church.

**Justice Carmon** lives in Wheaton, Illinois. He teaches weekly at the DuPage County Jail, gathering monthly with Christian artists, and traveling yearly as a short-term missionary to the distant lands of Russia, Kazakhstan, India, and Seattle.

**Judith Costello** grew up as one of six children in Davenport, Iowa. Now she has a family of her own in rural New Mexico. Judith writes for many national publications when she is not teaching art and Sunday school.

**Nina Edwards** currently serves as the National Director of Staff and Volunteer Development for Youth for Christ/USA in Denver. She has been in youth ministry for 22 years and is passionate about following Jesus, loving kids, and developing people. Her favorite role is aunt to 10 nieces and nephews.

**Julie Grimes** is an award-winning journalist who lives in Indianapolis with her husband and four children. She is currently writing a book on Christian leaders.

**Justin Hanselman** resides in the suburbs of Chicago where he is a high school student. He has been writing since first grade and is increasingly interested in writing ironic and observational literature.

**Phyllis Harmony** is a speaker and author who travels the country sharing about the impact of God's Word on the common stuff of everyday life.

**Margaret Henry** was born and reared in Dallas. She earned an M.A. in educational ministries at Wheaton College. After graduating she became the Director of Children's Ministries at Naperville Presbyterian Church in Naperville, Illinois. Married to Jason since 1995, Margaret is currently homeschooling her two children in Geneva, Illinois.

**Andrea Howard** is a college student who enjoys teaching Pre-K Sunday school, reading God's Word, and going on mission trips to places like Jamaica. She wants to major in either women's or children's ministry.

**Elizabeth Hubbard** was raised in Indianapolis and Naperville, Illinois. She is a graduate of Vanderbilt University, receiving degrees in English and Psychological Science. Elizabeth enjoys running and the outdoors and is passionate about writing fiction and poetry.

**Heidi J. Krumenauer** is a writer, speaker, author, and a contributor to several compilation books. She is the political action director for a Fortune 400 insurance company. Heidi resides in Stoughton, Wisconsin, with her husband, Jeff, and sons, Noah and Payton.

**Barbara Lewis** lives with her husband in New Hampshire, where she teaches energetic adolescents at Laconia Christian School. Although she loves to cook and crochet, her most creative projects have been her two children, both of whom work with young people.

**Linda MacKillop** is the mother of four sons and nearing the empty nest stage of life. She works as a freelance writer and enjoys writing fiction, nonfiction, and drama. Linda and her husband recently relocated from Virginia to the Chicago area where they love exploring the city and getting outdoors when the temperature rises above freezing.

**Danette Matty** has been a youth ministry volunteer since big hair was in. She's a freelance writer and speaker who contributes as a reviewer, youth worker correspondent, and author for several publications. She is the director of student ministries with Crew at Real Life Church in Minnesota, where she lives with her husband and favorite students—her two kids.

**Kim Moore** is a happily married mother of three children living in Corpus Christi, Texas. She has been an educator since 1991, currently teaching eighth grade math. In her free time she enjoys drama, reading, and writing.

**Mark R. Nesbitt** is the published author of numerous articles, educational materials, and books on a variety of topics. He had the unusual experience of actually enjoying high school, though perhaps it is only due to faulty or selective memory. He lives in the Chicago area with his wife and three children.

**Toni Peinado** lives in Albuquerque with her husband LeeRoy, her son, Nathan, a very fat yellow lab named Caytee, and Oliver, her skinny cat. She enjoys reading, watching movies, crafts, and anything fun.

**Heather Pleier** lives with her husband in Germany. Taking a break from teaching high school English, she enjoys writing and exploring the European countryside.

**Jeanine Pynes** is a spiritual director with the Navigatio Group, holds a M.A. in biblical counseling from Colorado Christian University and is a licensed professional counselor. Jeanine is married with a four-year-old daughter. She lives in Denver.

**Gene R. Smillie** is a cross-cultural educator and missionary. As a university professor and pastor, he has worked in Europe, Africa, and South America, and among a wide variety of cultures in North America.

**Carol Smith** is a freelance writer and songwriter living in Nashville in a fixer-upper home with two contented cats and two happy and large dogs.

**Sally Smith** is an inspirational speaker and freelance writer from southwest Missouri. She is the founder of New Beginning Ministries, which encourages women to grow in the grace and knowledge of Jesus. Sally, a former guidance counselor, and her husband were foster parents for troubled teenagers. They now parent two adopted children and a foreign exchange student from Mexico.

**Alene Snodgrass** is an author and speaker. As the director of SHE Fellowship at Christ Point Church in Corpus Christi, Texas. Her passion is to draw others to Christ and see lives change.

**Ruth Ann Somerville** grew up as the daughter of missionaries in South Korea. Now she makes her home in the beautiful mountains of North Carolina with her husband, Walter, and their three children.

**Gloria R. Spielman** has been married since 1983 and is the mother of two boys, one in college and one in middle school. She is a freelance writer, teaches women's Bible studies at her church, and sings on the church worship team. Her hobbies are working in her yard, maintaining a saltwater coral reef tank, playing hammered dulcimer and electric bass, reading classic mysteries, and studying Christian literature.

**Elisa Fryling Stanford** is a freelance author and editor. She lives in Colorado with her husband and daughter.

**Dennis Stout** is a youth pastor in the Kansas City area where he lives with his wife, Robin, and two children.

**Ronica Stromberg** keeps busy in the lives of her sons and squeezes in reading and writing whenever she can. She lives in Lincoln, Nebraska.

**Ann Swindell** is a writer who lives and works in the Chicago suburbs with her husband, Michael. A graduate of Wheaton College, she is currently working on her masters in writing at DePaul University.

**C. J. Sylraen** lived for 24 years in Southern California, 10 years in Japan, and the last three years in Illinois. Her love of different cultures and languages has led her to become a fantasy novel writer, where she can create her own worlds and pursue her passion for writing.

**Stephen Tracy** was born in Atlanta, but has spent the majority of his years in the Chicago area. Beyond his love of writing, he is also a gifted musician, who has written, performed, and recorded some of his original works. He is currently pursuing a double degree in English and Secondary Education.

**Tom Vick** is a freelance writer from West Chicago, Illinois. He enjoys playing football for Wheaton Academy High School and writing for the school's literary journal. His main goal in life is to glorify God through his writing and football.

**Tama Joy Westman,** a seasoned journalist and award-winning writer and editor, loves to capture the stories that can change lives. She lives in the Minneapolis area.

**Johannah Helen Wetzel** spent her childhood and teenage years in Cochabamba, Bolivia, where she loved hiking in the Andes Mountains. She is now enjoying living near the ocean in Vancouver, British Columbia, and working toward a master's degree in Spiritual Theology. She still loves to hike, but has traded in wearing funky pants for wearing funky scarves.

**Neil Wilson** lives in rural Wisconsin with his wife, Sherrie. Some of his best memories comes from 13 years' service in a country church in Eureka, Wisconsin. Neil has authored and contributed to numerous books and specialty Bibles produced by the Livingstone Corporation.

**Colleen J. Yang,** a former missionary to Japan, is a freelance writer and illustrator living in Carol Stream, Illinois, with her two children, Isaac and Lydia. She is fluent in Japanese and enjoys writing music.

**Karen Young** is a freelance writer who especially enjoys writing poetry. She was inspired as a child by the rich preaching, poetic, and music traditions of African American culture. In her leisure time, Karen also enjoys spending time with friends, singing, reading, and traveling.

**Betsy Zenz** is a freelance writer and editor. She lives in Boulder, Colorado, with her husband, Andy, and daughter, Mercy.

# TOPICAL INDEX

**Abandonment**
Not Finished Yet. . . . . . . . . . . . . . . . . 241
Peace as a Masterpiece . . . . . . . . . . . . . 18

**Abilities/Gifts, using**
A Reason to Play . . . . . . . . . . . . . . . 109
Birds Don't Gallop and
Horses Don't Sing . . . . . . . . . . . . . . . 85

**Abstinence**
Abstinence Road . . . . . . . . . . . . . . . 169

**Acceptance**
Cutting through the Pain . . . . . . . . . . . . 29
Harvesting Joy . . . . . . . . . . . . . . . . . 89

**Advice** (see *Guidance, needing or Wisdom*)

**Affirmation**
A Reason to Play . . . . . . . . . . . . . . . 109

**Anger**
A Change of Direction . . . . . . . . . . . . . 68
Dealing with Darkness . . . . . . . . . . . . 208
Does Jesus Really Love Me? . . . . . . . . 136

**Anorexia**
Peace as a Masterpiece . . . . . . . . . . . . . 18

**Baptism**
A Baptism of Rain . . . . . . . . . . . . . . . 64
An Attitude Adjustment . . . . . . . . . . . . 57
My Stepdad and Me . . . . . . . . . . . . . . 47

**Belonging**
Harvesting Joy . . . . . . . . . . . . . . . . . 89
The Way Less Traveled . . . . . . . . . . . . 74

**Bible, the (God's Word)/Bible Study**
A Baptism of Rain . . . . . . . . . . . . . . . 64
A Matter of Perspective . . . . . . . . . . . 230
Have You Ever Been in Love? . . . . . . . . 93
Wrestling with Faith . . . . . . . . . . . . . 140

**Bitterness/Resentment**
An Attitude Adjustment . . . . . . . . . . . . 57
Dealing with Darkness . . . . . . . . . . . . 208

**Body of Christ/Community of Believers/
the Church**
In This Together . . . . . . . . . . . . . . . . 144

Tomorrow's Choices Today . . . . . . . . . . 234

**Bulimia**
Does Jesus Really Love Me? . . . . . . . . 136

**Bullying**
The Lifting . . . . . . . . . . . . . . . . . . . 162

**Change/Transformation**
An Attitude Adjustment . . . . . . . . . . . . 57
Busy and Broken . . . . . . . . . . . . . . . 204
Burnt Shoes . . . . . . . . . . . . . . . . . . 193
Empty Stockings, Full Hearts . . . . . . . . 116
Harvesting Joy . . . . . . . . . . . . . . . . . 89
Shooting Basketballs, Not Bullets . . . . . 196

**Choices**
Busy and Broken . . . . . . . . . . . . . . . 204
Lost in God . . . . . . . . . . . . . . . . . . 190
Making Plans . . . . . . . . . . . . . . . . . 132
My Wake-Up Call . . . . . . . . . . . . . . . 43
The Great Date Wait . . . . . . . . . . . . . 223

**Commitment**
*to Jesus (Discipleship)*
A Baptism of Rain . . . . . . . . . . . . . . . 64
Abstinence Road . . . . . . . . . . . . . . . 169
Arms Wide Open . . . . . . . . . . . . . . . 200
Burnt Shoes . . . . . . . . . . . . . . . . . . 193
*to others*
Letting Go of Eric . . . . . . . . . . . . . . . 53
Not So Far Away . . . . . . . . . . . . . . . 154

**Compassion**
A Horse Story . . . . . . . . . . . . . . . . . 71
Happy New Year . . . . . . . . . . . . . . . 61
House of Hope . . . . . . . . . . . . . . . . 106
Sheep, Goats, and a Pair of Shoes . . . . . 82
The World's Worst Driver . . . . . . . . . . . 35
Wrestling with Faith . . . . . . . . . . . . . 140

**Conflict**
My Stepdad and Me . . . . . . . . . . . . . . 47
Not So Far Away . . . . . . . . . . . . . . . 154
Paid in Full . . . . . . . . . . . . . . . . . . . 39
The Raging Fire . . . . . . . . . . . . . . . . 32

**Cutting**
Cutting through the Pain . . . . . . . . . . . 29

**Dating**
Abstinence Road . . . . . . . . . . . . . . . . 169
The Great Date Wait . . . . . . . . . . . . . 223
*breakups of*
Busy and Broken . . . . . . . . . . . . . . . . 204
Have You Ever Been in Love? . . . . . . . . 93
My Wake-Up Call . . . . . . . . . . . . . . . . 43

**Death**
*of a parent or other significant person*
A Poolside Chat . . . . . . . . . . . . . . . . . 237
In This Together . . . . . . . . . . . . . . . . . 144
It's All True. . . . . . . . . . . . . . . . . . . . . 100
*of Jesus*
Peace as a Masterpiece . . . . . . . . . . . . . 18

**Depression/Discouragement/
Disappointment**
Cutting through the Pain . . . . . . . . . . . 29
Dealing with Darkness . . . . . . . . . . . . 208
Down and Out. . . . . . . . . . . . . . . . . . 219
Empty Stockings, Full Hearts . . . . . . . 116
Keep Going! . . . . . . . . . . . . . . . . . . . 227
So You Had a Bad Day . . . . . . . . . . . . . 26

**Discipline**
A Reason to Play . . . . . . . . . . . . . . . . 109
Ahead of the Game . . . . . . . . . . . . . . 165
Dealing with Darkness . . . . . . . . . . . . 208
Keep Going! . . . . . . . . . . . . . . . . . . . 227

**Divorce**
Down and Out. . . . . . . . . . . . . . . . . . 219
Not Finished Yet. . . . . . . . . . . . . . . . . 241
Not So Far Away . . . . . . . . . . . . . . . . 154
Paid in Full. . . . . . . . . . . . . . . . . . . . . 39
Who Is He? . . . . . . . . . . . . . . . . . . . . 112

**Doubts**
Does Jesus Really Love Me? . . . . . . . . . 136

**Drinking/Partying**
Busy and Broken . . . . . . . . . . . . . . . . 204
Down and Out. . . . . . . . . . . . . . . . . . 219
Not So Far Away . . . . . . . . . . . . . . . . 154

**Drugs**
Busy and Broken . . . . . . . . . . . . . . . . 204
Down and Out. . . . . . . . . . . . . . . . . . 219
Shooting Basketballs, Not Bullets . . . . . 196

**Evangelism**
A Baptism of Rain . . . . . . . . . . . . . . . . 64
A Musical Moment . . . . . . . . . . . . . . 184
Are You Qualified? . . . . . . . . . . . . . . . 172
Lip Service . . . . . . . . . . . . . . . . . . . . . 78
Shooting Basketballs, Not Bullets. . . . . 196

**Expectations**
Birds Don't Gallop and
Horses Don't Sing . . . . . . . . . . . . . . . . 85
Expectations. . . . . . . . . . . . . . . . . . . . . 14
Keep Going! . . . . . . . . . . . . . . . . . . . 227
Making It Right . . . . . . . . . . . . . . . . . . 22

**Failure/Making Mistakes**
A Change of Direction . . . . . . . . . . . . . 68
Birds Don't Gallop and
Horses Don't Sing . . . . . . . . . . . . . . . . 85
Keep Going! . . . . . . . . . . . . . . . . . . . 227
My Three Minutes of Glory . . . . . . . . . . 7
Taking the Heat . . . . . . . . . . . . . . . . . 147
The Grizzly and the
Air-Conditioner . . . . . . . . . . . . . . . . . 181
The World's Worst Driver. . . . . . . . . . . . 35

**Faith**
Burnt Shoes . . . . . . . . . . . . . . . . . . . 193
Empty Stockings, Full Hearts . . . . . . . 116
It's All True. . . . . . . . . . . . . . . . . . . . . 100
Keep Going! . . . . . . . . . . . . . . . . . . . 227
Lip Service . . . . . . . . . . . . . . . . . . . . . 78
My Stepdad and Me. . . . . . . . . . . . . . . 47
The "Boring" Life. . . . . . . . . . . . . . . . 187
The Real Deal. . . . . . . . . . . . . . . . . . . . 97
Wrestling with Faith . . . . . . . . . . . . . . 140

**Family**
An Attitude Adjustment. . . . . . . . . . . . 57
Dealing with Darkness . . . . . . . . . . . . 208
My Stepdad and Me. . . . . . . . . . . . . . . 47

**Forgiveness/Reconciliation**
Busy and Broken . . . . . . . . . . . . . . . . 204
Fear Has a Purpose. . . . . . . . . . . . . . . 179
Making It Right . . . . . . . . . . . . . . . . . . 22
My Wake-Up Call . . . . . . . . . . . . . . . . 43
Paid in Full. . . . . . . . . . . . . . . . . . . . . 39
The Grizzly and the
Air-Conditioner . . . . . . . . . . . . . . . . . 181

**Friendship**
A Poolside Chat . . . . . . . . . . . . . . . . . 237
Letting Go of Eric . . . . . . . . . . . . . . . 53
Lost in God . . . . . . . . . . . . . . . . . . . . 190

**Future, plans for**
A Change of Direction . . . . . . . . . . . . 68
A Whole New Dream . . . . . . . . . . . . 175
Dealing with Darkness . . . . . . . . . . . . 208
Expectations. . . . . . . . . . . . . . . . . . . . 14
Making Plans . . . . . . . . . . . . . . . . . . 132

**Gang Involvement**
Shooting Basketballs, Not Bullets . . . . . 196

**God**
*Fatherhood of*
Who Is He? . . . . . . . . . . . . . . . . . . . 112

*help from/provision of*
A Horse Story. . . . . . . . . . . . . . . . . . . 71
Down and Out. . . . . . . . . . . . . . . . . . 219
Empty Stockings, Full Hearts . . . . . . . 116
Expectations. . . . . . . . . . . . . . . . . . . . 14
Paid in Full. . . . . . . . . . . . . . . . . . . . 39
So You Had a Bad Day . . . . . . . . . . . . 26

*peace of*
Have You Ever Been in Love? . . . . . . . . 93
Not So Far Away . . . . . . . . . . . . . . . . 154
Peace as a Masterpiece . . . . . . . . . . . . 18

*plans/will of*
A Matter of Perspective . . . . . . . . . . . 230
A Whole New Dream . . . . . . . . . . . . 175
Happy New Year . . . . . . . . . . . . . . . . 61
The Great Date Wait . . . . . . . . . . . . . 223

*presence of*
A Baptism of Rain . . . . . . . . . . . . . . . 64
Ahead of the Game . . . . . . . . . . . . . . 165
God in the Bullring . . . . . . . . . . . . . . 128
In This Together. . . . . . . . . . . . . . . . . 144
Not Finished Yet. . . . . . . . . . . . . . . . 241

*protection of*
My Stepdad and Me . . . . . . . . . . . . . . 47

*strength of*
Birds Don't Gallop and
Horses Don't Sing . . . . . . . . . . . . . . 85

**Gossip/Rumors, dealing with**
My Stepdad and Me . . . . . . . . . . . . . . 47
Peace as a Masterpiece . . . . . . . . . . . . 18
The Raging Fire . . . . . . . . . . . . . . . . . 32

**Grief/Coping**
A Horse Story. . . . . . . . . . . . . . . . . . . 71
Cutting through the Pain . . . . . . . . . . 29
Dealing with Darkness . . . . . . . . . . . . 208
It's All True. . . . . . . . . . . . . . . . . . . . 100
In This Together. . . . . . . . . . . . . . . . . 144

**Guidance, needing**
A Change of Direction . . . . . . . . . . . . 68
Are You Qualified? . . . . . . . . . . . . . . 172
Expectations. . . . . . . . . . . . . . . . . . . . 14
Taking the High Road . . . . . . . . . . . . 151
The Great Date Wait . . . . . . . . . . . . . 223
View from the Bench . . . . . . . . . . . . . 11
Who Is He? . . . . . . . . . . . . . . . . . . . 112

**Hardship/Disaster**
Down and Out. . . . . . . . . . . . . . . . . . 219
Empty Stockings, Full Hearts . . . . . . . 116
House of Hope. . . . . . . . . . . . . . . . . . 106
The Way Less Traveled . . . . . . . . . . . . 74

**Heaven/God's Kingdom**
Busy and Broken . . . . . . . . . . . . . . . . 204
It's All True. . . . . . . . . . . . . . . . . . . . 100
Lip Service . . . . . . . . . . . . . . . . . . . . 78
Sheep, Goats, and a Pair of Shoes . . . . . . 82

**Homosexuality**
Tomorrow's Choices Today. . . . . . . . . . 234

**Hope**
House of Hope. . . . . . . . . . . . . . . . . . 106
Lost in God . . . . . . . . . . . . . . . . . . . . 190

**Humility/Humiliation**
A Lesson in Laughter . . . . . . . . . . . . . 216
An Embarrassing Moment . . . . . . . . . . 158
Down and Out. . . . . . . . . . . . . . . . . . 219
Empty Stockings, Full Hearts . . . . . . . 116
Invisible . . . . . . . . . . . . . . . . . . . . . . 212
The World's Worst Driver. . . . . . . . . . . 35
Who Am I? . . . . . . . . . . . . . . . . . . . . 124

**Jesus**

*compassion of*
A Horse Story . . . . . . . . . . . . . . . . . . . 71

*faithfulness of*
My Wake-Up Call . . . . . . . . . . . . . . . 43

*honoring*
A Drive to Remember . . . . . . . . . . . . 50

*humanity of*
A Horse Story . . . . . . . . . . . . . . . . . . . 71

*presence of*
A Musical Moment . . . . . . . . . . . . . . 184

**Joy**
A Reason to Play . . . . . . . . . . . . . . . . 109
Harvesting Joy . . . . . . . . . . . . . . . . . . 89

**Judging others**
Down and Out . . . . . . . . . . . . . . . . . . 219
Making It Right . . . . . . . . . . . . . . . . . 22
Wrestling with Faith . . . . . . . . . . . . . 140

**Leadership**
Ahead of the Game . . . . . . . . . . . . . . 165
Tomorrow's Choices Today . . . . . . . . 234

**Loneliness**
Abstinence Road . . . . . . . . . . . . . . . . 169
Lost in God . . . . . . . . . . . . . . . . . . . . 190

**Love**

*of God/Jesus*
An Embarrassing Moment . . . . . . . . . 158
Cutting through the Pain . . . . . . . . . . 29
Letting Go of Eric . . . . . . . . . . . . . . . 53
Who Am I? . . . . . . . . . . . . . . . . . . . . 124

*for others*
Have You Ever Been in Love? . . . . . . . 93

*heartache of*
Letting Go of Eric . . . . . . . . . . . . . . . 53

*showing God's*
A Coyote for Christmas . . . . . . . . . . . 120
An Embarrassing Moment . . . . . . . . . 158

**Meaning/Relevance**
A Matter of Perspective . . . . . . . . . . . 230

**Misconceptions**
*about God*

Does Jesus Really Love Me? . . . . . . . . 136
Invisible . . . . . . . . . . . . . . . . . . . . . . . 212
Not Finished Yet . . . . . . . . . . . . . . . . 241

*about people*
A Lesson in Laughter . . . . . . . . . . . . . 216
Letting Go of Eric . . . . . . . . . . . . . . . 53

**Mocking Others**
A Lesson in Laughter . . . . . . . . . . . . . 216

**Music**
A Musical Moment . . . . . . . . . . . . . . 184
A Reason to Play . . . . . . . . . . . . . . . . 109
Arms Wide Open . . . . . . . . . . . . . . . . 200

**Obedience**
A Drive to Remember . . . . . . . . . . . . 50
Are You Qualified? . . . . . . . . . . . . . . . 172
Lost in God . . . . . . . . . . . . . . . . . . . . 190
The "Boring" Life . . . . . . . . . . . . . . . . 187

**Overcoming Adversity**
My Three Minutes of Glory . . . . . . . . . . 7

**Pain**

*emotional*
Cutting through the Pain . . . . . . . . . . 29
Not So Far Away . . . . . . . . . . . . . . . . 154
Peace as a Masterpiece . . . . . . . . . . . . 18
The Way Less Traveled . . . . . . . . . . . . 74

*physical*
A Horse Story . . . . . . . . . . . . . . . . . . . 71
Cutting through the Pain . . . . . . . . . . 29
God in the Bullring . . . . . . . . . . . . . . 128
Not So Far Away . . . . . . . . . . . . . . . . 154

**Parents/Stepparents**

*difficult relationships with*
My Stepdad and Me . . . . . . . . . . . . . . 47

*failure of*
Not Finished Yet . . . . . . . . . . . . . . . . 241
Paid in Full . . . . . . . . . . . . . . . . . . . . 39

*illness of*
A Coyote for Christmas . . . . . . . . . . . 120

**Perfection, true**
Peace as a Masterpiece . . . . . . . . . . . . 18

**Perseverance/Persistence**
Birds Don't Gallop and
Horses Don't Sing . . . . . . . . . . . . . . . 85
Keep Going! . . . . . . . . . . . . . . . . . . . . 227
My Three Minutes of Glory . . . . . . . . . . 7

**Popularity**
A Lesson in Laughter . . . . . . . . . . . . . 216
An Embarrassing Moment . . . . . . . . . 158
Busy and Broken . . . . . . . . . . . . . . . . 204

**Prayer**
Are You Qualified? . . . . . . . . . . . . . . . 172
Arms Wide Open . . . . . . . . . . . . . . . 200
Cutting through the Pain . . . . . . . . . . . 29
Expectations . . . . . . . . . . . . . . . . . . . . . 14
God in the Bullring . . . . . . . . . . . . . . 128
My Three Minutes of Glory . . . . . . . . . . 7
Not So Far Away . . . . . . . . . . . . . . . . 154
Paid in Full . . . . . . . . . . . . . . . . . . . . . 39
So You Had a Bad Day . . . . . . . . . . . . . 26
Who Is He? . . . . . . . . . . . . . . . . . . . . 112

**Pregnancy**
Making It Right . . . . . . . . . . . . . . . . . . 22
My Wake-Up Call . . . . . . . . . . . . . . . . 43

**Pride**
Dealing with Darkness . . . . . . . . . . . . 208
Down and Out . . . . . . . . . . . . . . . . . . 219
Who Am I? . . . . . . . . . . . . . . . . . . . . 124

**Rejection**
Birds Don't Gallop and
Horses Don't Sing . . . . . . . . . . . . . . . 85
Have You Ever Been in Love? . . . . . . . . 93
Keep Going! . . . . . . . . . . . . . . . . . . . . 227
Letting Go of Eric . . . . . . . . . . . . . . . . 53
Making Plans . . . . . . . . . . . . . . . . . . . 132
The Great Date Wait . . . . . . . . . . . . . 223

**Repentance**
Arms Wide Open . . . . . . . . . . . . . . . 200
Busy and Broken . . . . . . . . . . . . . . . . 204
Fear Has a Purpose . . . . . . . . . . . . . . . 179

**Restoration**
Happy New Year . . . . . . . . . . . . . . . . . 61
Not So Far Away . . . . . . . . . . . . . . . . 154

**Sex/Sexuality**
Abstinence Road . . . . . . . . . . . . . . . . 169
Busy and Broken . . . . . . . . . . . . . . . . 204
Making It Right . . . . . . . . . . . . . . . . . . 22
My Wake-Up Call . . . . . . . . . . . . . . . . 43

**Sin**
Busy and Broken . . . . . . . . . . . . . . . . 204
Making It Right . . . . . . . . . . . . . . . . . . 22

**Spiritual Thirst**
In Search of Water . . . . . . . . . . . . . . . 103

**Suicide**
Dealing with Darkness . . . . . . . . . . . . 208
Not So Far Away . . . . . . . . . . . . . . . . 154

**Taking Responsibility**
Not Finished Yet . . . . . . . . . . . . . . . . 241
Taking the Heat . . . . . . . . . . . . . . . . . 147

**Thankfulness**
Empty Stockings, Full Hearts . . . . . . . 116
Making It Right . . . . . . . . . . . . . . . . . . 22

**Trusting God**
A Lesson in Laughter . . . . . . . . . . . . . 216
Are You Qualified? . . . . . . . . . . . . . . . 172
God in the Bullring . . . . . . . . . . . . . . 128
Keep Going! . . . . . . . . . . . . . . . . . . . . 227
My Stepdad and Me . . . . . . . . . . . . . . . 47
Taking the High Road . . . . . . . . . . . . 151
The Lifting . . . . . . . . . . . . . . . . . . . . . 162

**Waiting**
It's All True . . . . . . . . . . . . . . . . . . . . 100
Making Plans . . . . . . . . . . . . . . . . . . . 132
The Great Date Wait . . . . . . . . . . . . . 223

**Wisdom/Wise Counsel**
View from the Bench . . . . . . . . . . . . . . 11

**Words, danger of**
The Raging Fire . . . . . . . . . . . . . . . . . . 32

**Worship**
A Musical Moment . . . . . . . . . . . . . . 184
Arms Wide Open . . . . . . . . . . . . . . . 200

# SCRIPTURE INDEX

**Genesis 16**
Not So Far Away . . . . . . . . . . . . . . . 154

**Genesis 16:13**
Not So Far Away . . . . . . . . . . . . . . . 154

**Genesis 21**
Not So Far Away . . . . . . . . . . . . . . . 154

**Exodus 33:14**
Dealing with Darkness . . . . . . . . . . . 208

**Deuteronomy 32:2**
A Baptism of Rain . . . . . . . . . . . . . . . 64

**Joshua 1:5, 9**
A Drive to Remember . . . . . . . . . . . . 50

**Joshua 1:9**
Ahead of the Game . . . . . . . . . . . . . 165

**1 Samuel 3**
Who Is He? . . . . . . . . . . . . . . . . . . 112

**1 Kings 19**
Dealing with Darkness . . . . . . . . . . . 208

**Psalm 3:3**
The Lifting . . . . . . . . . . . . . . . . . . . 162

**Psalm 9:10**
Have You Ever Been in Love? . . . . . . . 93

**Psalm 18:29**
Have You Ever Been in Love? . . . . . . . 93

**Psalm 18:36**
Taking the High Road . . . . . . . . . . . 151

**Psalm 22:1–4**
Not Finished Yet . . . . . . . . . . . . . . . 241

**Psalm 31:14**
My Stepdad and Me . . . . . . . . . . . . . 47

**Psalm 32:8**
A Whole New Dream . . . . . . . . . . . . 175

**Psalm 33:18**
House of Hope . . . . . . . . . . . . . . . . 106

**Psalm 34:19**
Have You Ever Been in Love? . . . . . . . 93

**Psalm 38:8–9**
Dealing with Darkness . . . . . . . . . . . 208

**Psalm 41:11**
The Lifting . . . . . . . . . . . . . . . . . . . 162

**Psalm 42**
Empty Stockings, Full Hearts . . . . . . . 116

**Psalm 42:11**
Empty Stockings, Full Hearts . . . . . . . 116

**Psalm 55:22**
Have You Ever Been in Love? . . . . . . . 93

**Psalm 81:10**
Busy and Broken . . . . . . . . . . . . . . . 204

**Psalm 102:7**
Lost in God . . . . . . . . . . . . . . . . . . 190

**Psalm 106:4**
A Matter of Perspective . . . . . . . . . . 230

**Psalm 107:31, 35**
Letting Go of Eric . . . . . . . . . . . . . . 53

**Psalm 111:10**
View from the Bench . . . . . . . . . . . . 11

**Psalm 119:33–35**
A Drive to Remember . . . . . . . . . . . . 50

**Psalm 119:51**
A Matter of Perspective . . . . . . . . . . 230

**Psalm 119:63**
Lost in God . . . . . . . . . . . . . . . . . . 190

**Psalm 119:105**
Taking the High Road . . . . . . . . . . . 151

**Psalm 126:5–6**
Harvesting Joy . . . . . . . . . . . . . . . . 89

**Psalm 139:1–3**
Invisible . . . . . . . . . . . . . . . . . . . . 212

**Psalm 139:14**
Cutting through the Pain . . . . . . . . . . 29

**Psalm 139:15–16**
Birds Don't Gallop and Horses Don't Sing . . . 85

**Proverbs 3:1–2**
Shooting Basketballs, Not Bullets . . . . . 196

**Proverbs 3:5–6**
A Change of Direction . . . . . . . . . . . . 68

**Proverbs 16:6**
Fear Has a Purpose. . . . . . . . . . . . . . . 179

**Proverbs 16:9**
Making Plans. . . . . . . . . . . . . . . . . . 132

**Proverbs 18:24**
A Poolside Chat . . . . . . . . . . . . . . . . 237

**Proverbs 19:21**
A Whole New Dream. . . . . . . . . . . . 175

**Proverbs 21:23**
The Raging Fire . . . . . . . . . . . . . . . . . 32

**Ecclesiastes 1:17**
Who Am I? . . . . . . . . . . . . . . . . . . . 124

**Isaiah 1:18**
My Wake-Up Call . . . . . . . . . . . . . . . 43

**Isaiah 26:3**
Have You Ever Been in Love? . . . . . . . . 93

**Isaiah 40:31**
House of Hope. . . . . . . . . . . . . . . . . 106

**Isaiah 43:2**
Taking the Heat . . . . . . . . . . . . . . . . 147

**Isaiah 43:18–19**
A Change of Direction. . . . . . . . . . . . . 68

**Isaiah 49:15**
Paid in Full. . . . . . . . . . . . . . . . . . . . 39

**Isaiah 55:3**
Busy and Broken . . . . . . . . . . . . . . . 204

**Isaiah 58:11**
The Great Date Wait . . . . . . . . . . . . . 223

**Jeremiah 29:11**
House of Hope. . . . . . . . . . . . . . . . . 106
Making Plans. . . . . . . . . . . . . . . . . . 132

**Lamentations 3:25**
House of Hope. . . . . . . . . . . . . . . . . 106

**2:22**
Who Is He? . . . . . . . . . . . . . . . . . . . 112

**3**
Taking the Heat . . . . . . . . . . . . . . . . 147

with Darkness. . . . . . . . . . . . 208

**Matthew 5:3**
The Way Less Traveled . . . . . . . . . . . . 74

**Matthew 5:8**
A Baptism of Rain . . . . . . . . . . . . . . . 64

**Matthew 7:1–3**
Wrestling with Faith. . . . . . . . . . . . . 140

**Matthew 16:24**
Arms Wide Open. . . . . . . . . . . . . . . 200

**Matthew 18:23–35**
Paid in Full. . . . . . . . . . . . . . . . . . . . 39

**Matthew 25:37–40**
Sheep, Goats, and a Pair of Shoes. . . . . . 82

**Matthew 28:20**
God in the Bullring . . . . . . . . . . . . . 128

**Mark 8:27–29**
Does Jesus Really Love Me? . . . . . . . . 136

**Mark 8:35**
Happy New Year . . . . . . . . . . . . . . . . 61

**Luke 3:22**
Who Am I? . . . . . . . . . . . . . . . . . . . 124

**Luke 12:24**
So You Had a Bad Day. . . . . . . . . . . . . 26

**Luke 12:48**
Shooting Basketballs, Not Bullets. . . . . 196

**John 1:12, 3:16**
Who Am I? . . . . . . . . . . . . . . . . . . . 124

**John 4:13–14**
In Search of Water . . . . . . . . . . . . . . 103

**John 8:10–11**
Making It Right . . . . . . . . . . . . . . . . . 22

**John 11:35**
A Horse Story. . . . . . . . . . . . . . . . . . 71

**John 14:1**
Have You Ever Been in Love? . . . . . . . . 93

**John 14:26**
Are You Qualified? . . . . . . . . . . . . . . 172

**Acts 16:16–40**
An Attitude Adjustment. . . . . . . . . . . . 57

**Romans 3:23**
The Grizzly and the Air-Conditioner . . 181

**Romans 5:15–16**
The Grizzly and the Air-Conditioner . . 181

**Romans 6:3**
An Attitude Adjustment . . . . . . . . . . . . 57

**Romans 8:1**
Making It Right . . . . . . . . . . . . . . . . . . 22

**Romans 8:18–25, 31–39**
Who Am I? . . . . . . . . . . . . . . . . . . . . 124

**Romans 8:38–39**
God in the Bullring . . . . . . . . . . . . . . 128

**Romans 12:3, 12**
A Lesson in Laughter . . . . . . . . . . . . . 216

**Romans 12:4–5, 15**
In This Together . . . . . . . . . . . . . . . . . 144

**Romans 12:9**
An Embarrassing Moment . . . . . . . . . . 158

**1 Corinthians 6:19–20**
Cutting through the Pain . . . . . . . . . . . 29

**1 Corinthians 10:13**
A Matter of Perspective . . . . . . . . . . . 230

**2 Corinthians 1:3–4**
The World's Worst Driver . . . . . . . . . . . 35

**2 Corinthians 12:8–9**
Who Is He? . . . . . . . . . . . . . . . . . . . . 112

**Galatians 2:20**
The "Boring" Life . . . . . . . . . . . . . . . . 187

**Galatians 5:13**
Shooting Basketballs, Not Bullets . . . . . 196

**Ephesians 1:13–14**
Who Am I? . . . . . . . . . . . . . . . . . . . . 124

**Ephesians 4:31**
Dealing with Darkness . . . . . . . . . . . . 208

**Philippians 1:6**
Making Plans . . . . . . . . . . . . . . . . . . . 132

**Philippians 1:23–24**
It's All True . . . . . . . . . . . . . . . . . . . . 100

**Philippians 3:12–16**
Keep Going! . . . . . . . . . . . . . . . . . . . 227

**Philippians 3:13–14**
Invisible . . . . . . . . . . . . . . . . . . . . . . 212

**Colossians 3:16**
A Musical Moment . . . . . . . . . . . . . . . 184

**1 Timothy 4:12**
Tomorrow's Choices Today . . . . . . . . . . 234

**Titus 2:6–7**
The Real Deal . . . . . . . . . . . . . . . . . . . 97

**Hebrews 4:15**
Abstinence Road . . . . . . . . . . . . . . . . 169

**Hebrews 4:15–16**
A Horse Story . . . . . . . . . . . . . . . . . . . 71

**Hebrews 10:14**
Peace as a Masterpiece . . . . . . . . . . . . 18

**Hebrews 11:1**
Burnt Shoes . . . . . . . . . . . . . . . . . . . 193

**Hebrews 12:5–11**
A Reason to Play . . . . . . . . . . . . . . . . 109

**Hebrews 13:8**
A Matter of Perspective . . . . . . . . . . . 230

**James 1:5–7**
Expectations . . . . . . . . . . . . . . . . . . . . 14

**James 1:17**
A Coyote for Christmas . . . . . . . . . . . 120

**James 2:14–17**
Lip Service . . . . . . . . . . . . . . . . . . . . . 7

**James 5:11**
My Three Minutes of Glory . . . . . . . .

**1 Peter 1:3**
House of Hope . . . . . . . . . . . . . . . . .

**1 Peter 5:6**
Down and Out . . . . . . . . . . . . . . . .